Chasing
Freedom with
America's Nomads

DIRTY
KIDS

GREYSTONE BOOKS

Vancouver/Berkeley

Greystone Books Ltd.
www.greystonebooks.com

Cataloguing data available from Library and Archives Canada
ISBN 978-1-77164-304-7 (pbk.)
ISBN 978-1-77164-306-1 (epub)

Editing by Jennifer Croll
Copyediting by Shirarose Wilensky
Proofreading by Paula Ayer
Cover design by Peter Cocking
Text design by Nayeli Jimenez
Cover and interior photographs by Kitra Cahana
Printed and bound in Canada on ancient-forest-friendly paper by Friesens

Every reasonable attempt has been made to secure permissions for the
images in this book. Information that will allow the publisher to rectify
any credit is welcome.

We gratefully acknowledge the support of the Canada Council for the
Arts, the British Columbia Arts Council, the Province of British Columbia
through the Book Publishing Tax Credit, and the Government of Canada
for our publishing activities.

For Kuba.

CONTENTS

FOREWORD

HE SCARCEST AND most precious resource is not oil, gold, or water. It cannot be found in the ground, grown on farms, or manufactured in a laboratory. The thing, if we may call it a "thing," most crucial for the survival and prosperity of humanity is not a material substance at all. Instead, the rare resource upon which the fate of our civilization depends is sovereignty, an immaterial attribute that grants the possessor the power to make decisions and dictate how our communities shall live.

Sovereignty—like its sibling, power, and cousin, wealth—has a tendency to accrue to small numbers of people. Even in democracy, a system of government that was intended to fairly distribute sovereignty to the many rather than to the few, we find that the power to decide the rules of social life is not something that many people ever possess. We are often ruled over and rarely the ruler. Few of us have ever experienced the freedom of being sovereign.

The uneven distribution of sovereignty is the fundamental problem plaguing contemporary life. More than income inequality, the inequality of sovereignty is the motivating force behind social unrest. Protests in the streets are a symptom of the fact that the wrong people are enforcing decisions that affect us all. The essence of protest is a call for the redistribution of sovereignty.

Dirty Kids is a thought-provoking, vibrant, and essential memoir for diagnosing our times, because it gives us a fresh, and much-needed, perspective on the pursuit of sovereignty outside established channels.

What is at stake is the question of how to expand sovereignty, how to create real physical spaces—whether they be festivals in forests or gatherings in dilapidated houses—where the external political powers, the police, and the elected representatives lose their gravitas and a new decision-making power and a new social organization bubbles up from the ground. An important part of the answer is found in the wild cast of characters who animate this book.

One of the themes that recurs throughout Chris Urquhart's journey is "home." She voluntarily becomes houseless in search of home. There is a close relationship between sovereignty and home: within our homes, and when we feel at home, each of us is a sovereign. (This connection remains codified in the law of Belgium, for example, where police are barred from raiding private homes during the night in pursuit of criminal suspects. From 9 PM to 5 AM, the walls of these homes become a barrier to external power.) Early in her travels, Urquhart experiences this sense of sovereignty outside of a traditional house. She writes, "I feel, for a split second, like I am part of something. I feel like I'm home." And having experienced a self-governed community for the first time, Urquhart wonders if she should stop taking the antidepressants that have helped her cope with Babylon, the other reality most of us inhabit. "Maybe I should go off my meds... If there's any place to do it, I think this would be it," she confides in Kitra, her traveling companion.

The quest for home leads to sincere moments of transcendent joy. But it also results in a debilitating anxiety and paralyzing fear of violence. It is this tension between momentarily finding utopia and uncovering a longer-lasting unease that makes *Dirty Kids* honest and worth reading. This is not a sanitized picture designed to glorify destitute poverty or blindly celebrate life on the streets. The reader is not forced into becoming an oogle, the "derogative term for hanger-on hipsters who try to act tough like travelers but have money or homes and a whole other life." Instead, it is a truthful encounter with the limits of social and political possibility.

In her travels with the nomadic cultures of America, Urquhart reveals an alternate path to sovereignty—a sovereignty without power and wealth—at the same time as she questions whether it is viable. The travelers that Urquhart introduces us to grant the reader an insight into the precursor communities and experiments in temporary self-governance that profoundly influenced the consensus-based structure of revolutionary social movements like Occupy Wall Street. Those who experienced the autonomous encampments of Occupy will see many similarities in the Rainbow Gatherings, for example. And the radical, free nomadic culture that *Dirty Kids* documents is likely to continue shaping the form of social protests to come.

Ultimately, the question remains whether sovereignty without political power is possible and desirable. Are the brief moments of finding a joyful communal home in the forest worth the terrible anxiety of financial and physical precariousness? Is it possible to conceive of a permanent sovereignty without power, a lasting ecstasy of belonging that does not come with painful anxiety? The value of *Dirty Kids* is that it provokes us to think about, and start talking about, these revolutionary questions.

In the final analysis, the only solution to the global challenges facing humanity—from catastrophic climate change to economic crisis—will be to solve the fundamental underlying problem of the scarcity of sovereignty. We must discover a way to multiply, and redistribute, sovereignty so that more of us have it and better decisions are being made. Reading *Dirty Kids* gives me hope. Chris Urquhart's memoir inspires me to believe that the people might be closer than ever to discovering the path to an abundance of sovereignty and a proliferation of joyous community.

MICAH WHITE, Co-Creator, Occupy, and author of *The End of Protest: A New Playbook for Revolution*

IIIIIIIIIIIIIIIIIIIIIIIIIIIIIIIIIIIIIII

Lady Liberty

I'VE SEEN LADY LIBERTY: she's knee-deep in your dumpster. Muscular arms, missing fingers: she's poetic, prophetic, and up close, she smells like pit bulls and powdered milk.

A dirty kid in Pennsylvania told me to avoid the seven-day itch: "The road's hard for the first seven days," he said. "It takes seven days to get used to it. But if you make it past the seven, then you're golden."

Itches plagued my entire trip.

I came into the world of travelers—runaways, Rainbows, Deadheads, and dropouts—as an absolute outsider. I was twenty-two and only ever had one family home. I tagged along with my best friend, photographer Kitra Cahana, who was twenty-one and had been traveling since she was in diapers. On assignment for the Italian magazine *COLORS*, we flew to the 2009 Rainbow Gathering in the Santa Fe National Forest in New Mexico, where we interviewed teenage runaways. What we found in Rainbowland warranted more than a five-hundred-word article. We continued to follow the story independently across the United States.

I traveled with American nomads on and off from 2009 to 2012. Kitra took photos and I recorded interviews. From the New Mexico Rainbow Gathering we hit the Pennsylvania regional Gathering, and then the Washington regional Gathering. In between these events, we lived and traveled with nomads in New York City, Ann Arbor, Detroit, New Orleans, Chattanooga, and Black Rock City, Nevada—the site of the Burning Man festival. For me, the journey that became this book ended at the 2012 Rainbow Gathering in Ocala, Florida, which I attended alone. Kitra still travels today.

Dirty Kids is a realistic, personal representation of U.S. transience, homelessness, and traveling culture. It is an ode to modern nomads, to those who move around constantly by choice or circumstance, to those who give us a living example of an alternative society. Some names have been changed.

CHAPTER 1

Welcome to Rainbowland

(JULY 2009)

SPLAYED ON A raggedy mattress in the back of a pickup truck I fake-smile, petrified. We're en route to Rainbowland, a festival I've never been to before, in a vehicle without seatbelts. A kid we just met a couple minutes ago, Sticky, is munching on garlic cloves beside me; he's tossing them into his beak like they're bubblegum. Sticky beams triumphantly. He's not the least bit self-conscious of his ripe bare feet or omnipresent body odor. He shouts blissfully out the window to no one in particular, long hair flowing biblically in the wind. "Lovin' you!" he says. "Lovin' you!"

I'm not sure where Kitra found this man, but he's hooked us up with a ride into Rainbowland. I trust Kitra without question. We're in New Mexico on assignment for an Italian magazine called *COLORS*: Kitra to take photos and me to write text and help carry gear. I've never been to a Rainbow Gathering before. Kitra has been to one in Israel. My bladder pinches, but I keep my mouth shut. I know I'm green—fresh meat.

"Coffee break!" shouts Amanda, the woman behind the wheel. "Everybody out!"

Amanda is a first-timer, too. She smiles defiantly. Her shirt reads: *International Indigenous Women's Day*.

We pick up more people along the way: Braham, a Robert Plant look-alike with a pill-white cast on his leg, and Jesse, a man in his twenties with a shaved head and expensive ball cap. When we pick up Jesse, Sticky jumps on him with a hug and yells, "Brother!" They're family from Rainbows past and are excited to have met up so serendipitously.

On the highway, Jesse sits too close to me on the communal mattress, adjusting his cap. He tells me about his work as a volunteer firefighter, how he hops from helicopters to extinguish roaring bush fires. My head jangles back and forth in the backseat. I keep my eyes on the horizon to avoid feeling nauseous.

"What're your chances of getting hurt?" I ask.

He says he doesn't know. I change the topic to Rainbowland, which is why I'm here. Jesse becomes very sentimental almost immediately. He tells me how he first got involved with the Family—the close network of Rainbow attendees.

"At fourteen I was on the streets. I could have gone down some really bad paths," he tells me. "But Rainbow set me straight. Actually, Rainbow saved my fucking life."

Soon, Jesse is inviting me to move into his yurt in Northern California, to live with him, off the land on his off-the-grid property. "I came to this Gathering to find a Sagittarius girl like you," he tells me. "Libra and Sagittarius are the perfect match, you know."

"Kitra's a Libra," I reply awkwardly, kicking the communal mattress. Kitra looks up from her camera screen, oblivious. She smiles, luminescent: long-limbed and starry-eyed, she snaps photos of the wacky foliage unfolding through our cracked windowpanes.

Two months earlier, I'd graduated from McGill University in Montreal, where I'd majored in anthropology and world religions. While there, I devoured ethnographies detailing the cultural customs of the African Nuer, the cheese-making techniques of the Persian Basseri, and the cultural customs of the Nuer of Sudan and the Sarakatsani of Greece. But it wasn't enough for me. I wanted to understand the nomadic cultures of my own continent, from my own perspective.

I'd met Kitra at McGill in an experimental religion class. Our professor, who insisted we refer to him by the moniker Lumière, was a tall, balding man with an ineffable spirit. In a stuffy school hell-bent on pomp and circumstance, he played the Pink Floyd song "Another Brick in the Wall" full blast at the beginning of each and every one of our lectures. He forced us up onto our feet to march in unison with our classmates, encouraging us to sing along with the lyrics, which he provided to us on paper.

Kitra, wearing an oversized shirt and dark glasses, sat in front of me on our first day. I told her I liked her top because I wanted to talk to her. She thanked me in her soft, solemn voice, saying she thought it might be her sister's.

"We don't really have our own clothes," she told me. "We just have a pile we all share."

This idea was so foreign to me. My WASP upbringing demanded we all have our own belongings, our own deep closets.

Lumière insisted each of us go by our own monikers. Kitra chose the name Dogmeta 95, in homage to director Lars von Trier's film movement, and I called myself Lady X, which I think was a vague reference to Sylvia Plath's "Lady Lazarus" mashed up with Bowie's "Lady Stardust." We really didn't think them through. At the end of class, Lumière told us we would go by those names, and those names only, until the end of the semester. So, we did.

In Lumière's class, I learned about Kitra's photography and career as an artist. She told me about her experiences as a teenager: photographing the Gaza Strip and landing her photo on the front cover of the *New York Times*, working as an assistant for a celebrity photographer in New York City. I was in immediate awe of her. To my delight, we quickly became inseparable. We started collaborating on stories to pass the time, traveling to London, Ontario, to cover an LGBTQ2 prom and to Coney Island to interview carnival workers. This collaboration would eventually lead us to Rainbowland.

The university fired Lumière a year later, which was a real shame, as his class was the most valuable one I took at McGill.

AS WE APPROACH the Santa Fe National Forest in northern New Mexico, the road turns to gravel soup. Cars line the roadsides like stubble: Volkswagen vans, Hondas, BMWs, and multitudes of multicolored school buses. Plates hail from Minnesota, South Dakota, New York, Nebraska, and beyond. Bumper stickers scream: *QUESTION REALITY, ARMS ARE FOR HUGGING, VIETNAM VET ON BOARD*, and *PEACE: BACK BY POPULAR DEMAND*. A few cars lie upside down in the ditch, having toppled over after being parked on shifting ground.

Amanda drives, slower now. From the window, I spy shoeless children, tattooed men sitting shirtless in lawn chairs.

"Welcome home!" Sticky shouts, still beaming.

"Lovin' you!" a man yells back from the road.

I'm overwhelmed by the call and response, by the oddities surrounding our vehicle—the clanking wheelbarrows, dilapidated buses—by the huge smiles everywhere I look. A young woman rides past our truck, bareback on a white stallion. She's carrying a newborn baby in a hand-sewn sling across her chest. I'm utterly awestruck, unable to speak. Kitra sits calmly, dreamily, waiting for the vehicle to come to a stop before exiting.

"It's a couple miles' hike to the site," Jesse says. "We'll carry those bags for you."

I spy a hand-cut path leading down a bank into wilderness. Sticky and Jesse grab our gear and tell us they'll come back for their own later.

THE FIRST OFFICIAL Gathering of the Rainbow Family of Living Light was held in 1972. The event, which took place in the Arapaho National Forest, Colorado, brought together more than twenty thousand Americans to live communally in the woods for more than a week. Their mission: to pray for world peace on the Fourth of July. Times have changed, but Rainbows, as the attendees are called, haven't stopped gathering since, in an unbroken chain of Gatherings, year after year. They build, operate, and then deconstruct a fully functioning temporary society in the middle of a national forest every summer.

Original Rainbow attendees were from a mishmash of subcultures: mainly hippies hell-bent on communal living, tripping flower children trailing off the '67 Summer of Love, Vietnam War protestors, Hells Angels bikers, and swaths of high school dropouts. Today, participants include homeless folks, crusty punks, and inner-city youth who come for the sense of community, free food, and stability the festival offers. Many homeless Rainbows make a life of jumping from Gathering to Gathering all year long. Gatherings have maintained popularity, with many events hosting more than thirty thousand participants. Regional Rainbows and international events occur throughout the year across the globe. Hippies are still the bread and butter of Rainbow culture, but because of its open, inclusive nature, Rainbowland is also a haven for people who just don't fit into the mainstream—poor Americans, those who have nothing to their name, full-time travelers, and teenage runaways. We're here to interview members of these last two groups.

THE ONLY PUBLISHED ethnography about Rainbowland is entitled *People of the Rainbow: A Nomadic Utopia* by Michael Niman.
In it, Niman attempts to explain the Family's population: "Some
members live under bridges, some in condominiums. For most,
the Gatherings are a vacation from Babylon, but for a dedicated
minority, Rainbow is a way of life." Babylon, I will soon learn, is
the term for society outside of Rainbowland. It's a catchall, not a
specific place on the map. Babylon is what traveling kids call any
town, city, or space outside of Rainbowland, any place that's not
"home."

In *All Ways Free*, the unofficial Rainbow Family newspaper,
the Gathering is described as a "diverse and decentralized social
fabric woven from the thread of hippie culture, back-to-land-ers,
American Indian spiritual teachings, pacifist-anarchist traditions,
eastern mysticism, and the legacy of the depression-era hobo
street wisdom."

Not everyone sees Rainbow in a positive light. The Depart-
ment of Homeland Security has named the Rainbow Family an
official "terrorist threat," a threat to national security. Local and
national police forces and park rangers spend thousands of dollars annually to monitor Gatherings—often much more money
than it takes to run the actual event. Since 1972, United States
government agencies have demanded to negotiate with leaders or spokespeople, but Rainbow only offers "liaisons" to aid
in conflict resolution. Legally, nobody is allowed to speak for
the Family—spokespeople, leaders, and presidents are not part
of this model. This means the police are unable to charge this
decentralized group of thousands of people for the organization
of the event, though local townships regularly attempt to take
legal action, and police presence at Gatherings is almost guaran-
teed. Despite this, Rainbows insistently continue exercising their
right to assemble on public land, to pray for peace on the Fourth
of July.

THE ROAD TO the main site is rough and bumpy. Handwritten signs hang limply from trees: *WE LOVE YOU, DOSE ME, FUCK UNCLE SAM, WELCOME HOME!* We pass bright eyes everywhere. I'm told the site was set up by Seed Camp—a group of the more hardcore Rainbows who come early to scout, clear, and maintain the site, and who stay late to return the land to its original form, ensuring the park environment is not compromised. Those involved in Seed Camp are often regular Rainbow attendees who spend weeks or months in the woods.

After half an hour's hike we reach Main Meadow, the center, or town square, of Rainbowland. Main Meadow is where the annual Prayer for Peace is held—the central event of this Gathering, a tradition carried on from the very first Gathering. This is where thousands will gather and pray on the Fourth. I look out at the large plain of burnt grass, almost as big as a football field, which holds hundreds of humans sitting in shapes, strumming instruments, reading books and manifestos, writing poetry, hula-hooping, and practicing devil sticks. There is an ever-present unyielding and ominous drum heartbeat. Hand-forged paths cover the periphery of the meadow, trails to hundreds of Rainbow kitchens, hidden in the woods. Some Rainbows have been on the site for weeks already, and the excitement is only ramping up as more people arrive.

"Hell yeah," Jesse shouts. "Welcome home!"

A hand-built information booth—a tiny, creaky hut—sits at one side of Main Meadow, where Main Circle, the Prayer for Peace on the Fourth, is held. Inside are handwritten maps of this year's setup, ride-share boards, schedules for free skill-share workshops, and a big box of clothes with a sign reading *FREE.*

"Where's Shtetl Kettle this year?" Sticky asks a man attending the booth.

Sticky's looking for a kosher kitchen that he's camped at before; the same kitchens appear year after year at Gatherings.

Young travelers congregate at Dirty Kids Camp, one of the darker dwellings in Rainbowland, to share smokes, rats, and guitar riffs.

NEW MEXICO, JULY 2009

He's told they aren't here this year, but the man suggests he try Turtle Soup instead. Swapping camps is a common occurrence; kitchens change, evolve, and swallow one another whole. Jesus Camp, Montana Mud, River Rats, Lovin' Ovens, Death Camp, Fat Kids Kitchen, and Shut Up and Eat It: Rainbow kitchens of various names feed thousands of Family members a day, all for free. In fact, everything in Rainbowland is free. Supplies are donated, forged, or "liberated" from the local town dumpsters (often to the dismay or, at times, sheer delight of the surrounding townships). There are long-standing camps that are generally in attendance at annual Gatherings, but Rainbows always adapt, moving, shifting. Kitra and I are on the search for a kosher vegetarian kitchen as well, so we follow Sticky.

"Seven up!" I hear a voice call through the forest.

Then I spy a congregation of police officers and park rangers on horseback passing through. The call amplifies as soon as it's heard, echoed by all Rainbows in earshot. This is a warning I will hear whenever police or park rangers are spotted in Rainbowland, a reminder that Babylonians are present and watching.

ON THE PATH to Turtle Soup we pass by the Trade Circle, a strip of forestland filled with small stalls and blankets bearing goods. The Trade Circle is where all commerce at the Gathering takes place, based solely on trade and barter. I spy muskrat furs; kombucha SCOBYs, the starter cultures that transform sweet tea into tangy, fizzy kombucha; collections of POG caps from the nineties fad game; and pocketknives. Rainbow kids collecting Grateful Dead stickers shout around me, unsupervised.

When we reach Turtle Soup, there are fifty or so tents sprawled around a communal fire pit. This is a kosher and vegan camp, and the smell of stewing legumes hangs heavy in the air, covering the crowd like a quilt. Tibetan prayer flags flap on trees, frantic squares of yellow, green, red, white, and blue. Scattered around the ground are a variety of figures, many with feathers in their hair and slim, precise physiques; everyone has excited eyes, and many clutch yoga mats. Twins with long black hair shred sheets of kale, ecstatic. In the "un-cooking area" of Turtle Soup, where the raw food is prepared, there's a hand-built wooden shack stocked with knives, bowls, and foodstuffs. A voice shouts from the kitchen, asking for volunteers, and a number of bodies rise from the dirt without a second's hesitation. This is how work gets done in Rainbowland: everyone volunteers their time to serve and help the Family.

I sit at the fire beside a chubby middle-aged man and listen to his conversation.

"I've been a punk rocker, a Hare Krishna, a shaman, a fanatical Jew. Rainbow people have seen me through my entire journey. They have accepted me no matter what I was."

I notice a kid riding a stationary bike, which appears to be rigged up to a blender.

"Walnut butter," someone whispers to me, noting my confused expression, and nods toward the mashed, nutty contents of the blender. "He's blending it by foot."

My mouth waters and I wait for dinner. I feel light, excitable, confused. I've never experienced such functional chaos, never witnessed such genuine social freedom.

AS A CHILD, I was taught to be suspicious of transient people. I remember an elementary school assembly, put on by the Toronto police: it was as an educational seminar warning children against the dangers of drug use. One cop was dressed up as a "street kid" called Shaggy; he wore rollerblades and a pink spiky wig. Shaggy shouted slogans to an audience of rapt eight-year-olds: he old us to stay away from pointy needles, and "being homeless stinks!" Even though I was young at the time, his performance always stuck with me. I never fully understood what was so bad about Shaggy's life: he had pink hair and sick rollerblades, and traveled around, living for free. He didn't have to go to school; he didn't have to wear what his parents told him to wear. What about his life stunk?

BEFORE TRAVELING TO Rainbowland, I had a dream I was Dean Moriarty from *On the Road*. In the dream, I crashed cars and owned my own chicken coop. I kept telling people I didn't want to be big or famous; I just wanted to "smell like life experience." I said it over and over again. I traveled with a Jack of sorts, a dream man who clung to me, tirelessly. He believed in me, wanted me to be a legend, but I didn't give a shit. I just crashed my cars and took care of my chickens. But, to be Dean, what a feeling: to be male and free and adored by everyone, to be American and insane and full of untethered energy! It was a good dream. But I woke up.

Kitra's awake beside me in our tent, poking at her camera again, shifting knobs. I've started to question whether she sleeps at all. Her presence is spectral, otherworldly, loving and calm. We discuss a plan of attack for the day: decide which camps to visit, what populations we should interview, how we should set up a portrait booth to meet incoming traveling teens. We zip our tent behind us as we leave and I worry about my belongings for a moment, then forget about it. There are no locked doors in Rainbowland.

We walk down the dirt path, lined with pebbles and brightly colored signs, until we reach a small, dry clearing. There sit two teenaged boys, soaking in the sun under a sagging fir tree. We smile at them and wave, and they instantly call us over.

"Hey, sisters! Come take a seat!"

I didn't think it would be this easy.

The boys, who tell us their names are Josh and Sal, sit in the field separating Montana Mud Camp from Dirty Kids Camp, two of the darker dwellings in Rainbowland. These camps, which often go by different names depending on who's running the kitchen, consist of a mishmash of busted tents, chained mutts, and fire pits. They cater largely to street kids, train hoppers, teenage runaways, and squatters. Known as Drainbows, the rough-edged members of these camps are often scrutinized by the more staunch and sober Family members who don't believe in drinking or drug use, including some of the folks back at Turtle Soup. Names like Nomad, Useless, and Clutter fill the air, bumping up against the scents of patchouli oil and gasoline. At times, I wonder if the teens are calling out to their friends or their pets. Face tattoos are plentiful.

We ask Sal and Josh about the instruments they're holding.

"Our band is called the 12 Shades of Schwilly Silly," Sal says, sauced and lusty. The tattoos on his knuckles read, *Voodoo Hand*. "'Schwilly' is that happy-silly drunk," he explains.

A lucky dollar bill is stitched to the side of Sal's bowler cap, crumpled and pretty like a green lily. Josh wears a frilly dress with filthy dreadlocks. We tell them why we're here and they seem unfazed, open, excited. After we've been sitting with them for a few minutes, Eli, another band member, arrives. He wears suspenders and a soiled striped shirt. He speaks softly, looking us in the eye, suspicious. Sal sucks on his rusty harmonica, and Josh begins to tap a sloppy beat on his "drum set"—a group of overturned buckets and cracked plastic pails. The threesome begins to belt out a soulful, upbeat song.

By noon, I lie in a puppy pile of teenagers. They are all under twenty-one and filthy as sin: with matted hair and bruise-colored tats, wearing rags and rats and crooked grins.

"We're going to be reincarnated," Sal sings, strumming wildly on his beat-up guitar, "reincarnated as birds."

Eli's voice, harsh and defiant, rips out of him like he's upchucking a steak. His torn patchwork pants are a barf of green corduroy, frayed denim, and dirty white lace. Beside him sits Elanor, who clutches her accordion: a black-and-white beast stuck shut with duct tape. She's soft-spoken but a bold singer, with bright, brassy brown dreadlocks. She yelps along to the song like a swallow hopping through a sewer. Sicka, also known as Jessika, a pale and sturdy redhead from Washington with a full-body sunburn, sits stoically, scowling at the crowd. A handful of silver piercings cling to her face. Like her, many Rainbows go by aliases, monikers, or self-chosen names. Many do this because they are running from the law, or for other personal reasons.

Sicka asks us what we're doing here, and we tell her we're working on an article about traveling teens at Rainbow. We've made a small photo album of Kitra's past work, shots from Kenya, Israel, and the Democratic Republic of the Congo. We pass it around the pile of kids, explaining that we want to travel with modern nomads. The kids shout emphatically, impressed, as most people are when they're confronted with Kitra's photography. Sicka flips through the pages, feigning disinterest. Dapper Dan, Sal's speckled mutt, coughs and licks an overturned can of beans. Bottles of Faygo soft drink and Jim Beam clink and plonk. Beside us, a young couple copulates openly in the dewy summer air.

I ask Sal for an interview and he agrees, graciously. He begins by telling me how he started traveling.

"I was a pretty confused youth... I never wanted to go to school, so I dropped out my senior year and took my GED [high school equivalency] test. I was kind of confused about what I wanted to pursue. I didn't know a school that would accept the GED besides a community college. I really wanted to get away from New York, just branch out and really discover who I was... so... I was reading a *Rolling Stone* magazine and I looked at the back and there's this [ad] for a school: Full Sail," he tells me.

"One of the things my mother was really pressuring me about was to get an education, go to school—she didn't have the opportunity to do so. She was a single mom and never had the time to go to school, so I kind of wanted to make her happy, and have a plan B, keep my options open. So I tried it out for four months. I really hated it. They were trying to sell this dream, and I didn't feel like they taught me enough skills or gave me enough individualized attention to obtain the thing that I wanted to accomplish—I didn't even know what I wanted to accomplish."

From this place of disillusionment Sal eventually stumbled into Rainbowland.

"It was just really random. I had been out of school one week, sitting in my apartment, depressed. Like, 'I don't want to go back to New York. There has to be another option.' I had never really been exposed to the traveling culture and didn't really know too much about it. I had met a bunch of kids living at the Rainbow Gathering in Ocala, Florida, when I was in Florida. My friend calls me up, like, 'Hey, these kids are staying above my friend's apartment. You should come down and meet them. I think you'd really vibe with them.' So we hung out, and they were like, 'Oh, we're going to Daytona Beach, then we're going to this festival in Miami, this Bob Marley tribute festival.' And so I was like, you know what? I have nothing going on, I have no obligations or anything tying me down to this place. Let's go! I went with them and was like, wow, I can live by just playing music and stuff. I always knew it was a possibility, but I never thought I could do it, so it was like really amazing to see these other kids' lifestyle. They really turned me onto something really amazing."

He giggles when I ask how his family responded to his choice.

"They thought I was absolutely insane. I come from a very traditional Roman Catholic Italian family. I don't want to say they're totally ignorant, but with certain things they have their own ideas and opinions, and can be closed minded and negative sometimes. So at first, they were like, 'You're going to be a bum?'"

I can relate to Sal's familial alienation. I think of my folks, not New York Catholics but Canadian WASPS. My parents, both high school teachers, always insisted on me having a bookish education, something I had pursued adamantly, tirelessly, yet fruitlessly, for most of my life. I'm curious about how Sal survives financially, tramping full time.

"It's easy to find shelter and it's easy to get around. Just stick out your thumb or hop a train," he informs me. "There's so much free food everywhere. I tell everyone if you go hungry in this country, you're missing some brain cells or just, like, totally lost. Because there is so much food that is thrown out and wasted. But the way I get money is through playing music—it's a pretty consistent way of having a little cash in my pocket. At least every time I play, I'll definitely get, like, twenty bucks. I can take myself out and get something warm and nice to eat, if I desire." He finishes, "People have this craft and this skill that they're able to share with other people and, you know, live a minimal lifestyle based on it. You know, you've got what you need and you don't really need anything else."

As he finishes, I think about the things back in my tent: Do I have everything I need to make it out here alone? I've never felt too attached to my possessions and hearing Sal's philosophy makes me feel lighter, optimistic.

DHARMA, A BUBBLY teen with a puffy lapdog named Dizzle, passes around a hand-rolled smoke, which is huffed by child hands. Beside her, her sister, Emma, sits scanning the horizon. Dharma's been traveling for years; although she's only nineteen, she tells me she's already been to thirty-eight of the fifty states.

"Dharma is my real name," she tells me. "It's not some hippie shit."

I want to know what she thinks about Rainbowland, why she comes to the Gatherings. She agrees to an interview.

"I see Rainbow as an accepting place. It doesn't really dis-criminate—and by 'doesn't discriminate' I mean it is accepting of people that you normally would not want to bring into your family," she tells me.

I ask her if she finds it lonely traveling by herself.

"As a girl I avoid traveling alone, just because I feel... I don't know. Every woman I've really ever loved or known very well has been hurt by a man sexually: my girlfriend, my sister, my mother. My mother was put into a mental hospital when she turned sixteen because she was raped. Back in the day, that was really, really, super taboo, and if you were willing to say some-thing about it, your family didn't want anybody knowing. They sent her away. Everyone I know has been hurt so much like that that I feel the need to protect myself. I carry big knives and I travel with people that I *trust* have my back."

Dizzle barks and Dharma continues, offering me her opin-ions on America. "I don't know a lot! I'm severely uneducated. I didn't go to high school. I just got really fucking high... I got a different type of education. But I know what I see. I observe the people around me, and I've been a lot of places in the United States. The people here have a lot of soul and a lot to give, and they just need a change—they just need some clarity. They need to give up a little bit of comfort. I've given up a whole lot of com-fort. I'll sleep on the hard ground, I'll sleep in the rain, I'll do what I gotta do, because it makes me happy to be free. You have to give up your comforts before you can really experience free-dom. You have to give up television, your favorite novel, your favorite whatever. You've got to give up your pillow."

Give up your pillow, I think to myself. *Give up your pillow.* This phrase bumps around in the back of my head. I grew up with clean sheets. I long for the freedom she describes.

MISTY DAWN AND Useless, Maria and Chris, and Viktoria and Dirty are tied at the wrists with string.

"Earth my body, water my blood, air my breath, and fire my spirit." We chant a pagan wedding prayer, led by a slouched Wiccan priest in a long purple robe.

Useless, one of the grooms, has spider web tattoos in his armpits, and Misty Dawn, his bride, has a face full of fishhooks. Viktoria, another bride, has short blonde hair and indentations burnt into her flesh: a triangle, a circle, and a square. Her soon-to-be hubby, Dirty, is shirtless in overalls. Maria and Chris have matching dreadlocks and huge grins. They pet their new kitten, tied to a string leash. All the couples beam brilliantly.

Wedding guests flood the open field. Word has gotten around that there's a photographer on-site, so Kitra has been asked to be the official wedding documentarian. She clicks away happily. Friends and strangers have woven handmade garlands from wild flowers, and the three brides wear floral wreaths in their hair. The couples head to the center of the field while the spectators, almost a hundred of us, form a perfect circle around them. The slouched Wiccan priest leads the whole event, which I learn is called a handfasting ceremony. He tells us to join hands and chant.

"Earth my body, water my blood, air my breath, and fire my spirit."

I hold the strangers' hands beside me, swaying awkwardly, smiling. A man in a wheelchair plucks at a tiny ukulele; another, younger man lies on the forest floor, shirtless, weeping uncontrollably in steampunk goggles. Children dip in and out of the circle, playing naked, unsupervised, ecstatic.

"Earth my body, water my blood, air my breath, and fire my spirit."

The priest smudges the couples with burning sage. He asks them to hop over a broom, and they do, two by two. Suddenly, the ceremony is completed and everyone raises their arms, elated.

"So mote it be," says the priest, and the lovers are wed among nature and madness.

Afterwards, there is a barbeque. Chicken breasts slathered with sugary brown sauce, and then delicious fat steaks once the larger crowd disperses. There is a huge chocolate wedding cake with thick buttercream. I wonder where they found or baked the cake—if they got ingredients in Babylon. The couples take turns feeding each other slices, shoving the brown sludge into each other's faces. Dirty and Viktoria grab handfuls, rambunctious, hurling it into the crowd. There is an air of exuberance and joy.

As the celebration unwinds, I spy a pair of goggles lying in the grass and pick them up. I look around and spot the weeping man I saw earlier. He seems more peaceful now, at ease, lying on the forest floor.

"I think you lost these," I say, and hand them to him.

He grabs the goggles without thanking me and introduces himself as Jimmy. Upon closer inspection, I realize he is also the man I saw having sex in the field even earlier, back at Dirty Kids Camp. He tells me he can read palms and I'm suddenly intrigued. He grabs my hand without asking and I don't complain, because I want to know more.

"You're a very sexual person," he tells me, his sooty finger snaking over my palm.

I pull back slightly, somewhat wary.

Sensing my unease, he laughs and refocuses. "Sorry," he says, stopping dramatically on one point on my hand. "Here is where you lose everything. Lose everything you thought you knew."

I raise an eyebrow.

Jimmy senses my distrust. He opens his own hand, calloused, scarred, suddenly shaking, and thrusts it toward me aggressively. "You don't believe me?" His wild eyes snap wide. He points to a deep groove near his thumb. "This is where my dad left." He points to another spot. "Here is where my best friend shot himself in the head." His eyes well up, wet and black, and he closes his hand, then stares at me. "It's not the circumference, it's the experience," he says.

Until this moment, my palm was a clumsy blob of flesh and fat. And now, it is a complicated road map to a bleak future. *Lose everything you thought you knew.*

"And you?" he adds, turning to Kitra, who is already walking back to Turtle Soup. "You walk with angels. You will always be safe."

I jog to catch up to her.

"MAYBE I SHOULD go off my meds," I tell Kitra when I wake up in the morning. I'm feeling invigorated. Being here has made me feel brave, able. "If there's any place to do it, I think this would be it."

"Okay," Kitra responds wearily. "But this might not be the best time."

Over the years, I've amassed a collection of medications for a number of ever-shifting diagnoses and psychiatric illnesses. I hated spending time sitting alone in psych wards, spilling my secrets to turned-off shrinks who wrote me endless scripts for anxiety medications. I hated being part of that scene but had no alternative, no other support where I came from other than pills, so I just swallowed them and tried to move forward.

But I don't question Kitra.

Mad folks frequent Rainbowland; "crazy" is not a bad word here, I've learned. Many Rainbows view their own diagnoses with skepticism. "Is there really something 'wrong' with me?" many Rainbows will ask. "Or is my anxiety an appropriate response to a broken system?" The Gathering is a great place to question Babylonian cultural and medical practices, and it provides a safe backdrop for this type of exploration. It's a place where the crazy come to play, often far away from worried or judgmental family members. But I'm here to observe and write, not participate, I remind myself, so I put my idea on the back burner.

Later, at Dirty Kids, I sit with Grace, a blonde girl with a lip ring. I'm interviewing her about her "crazy family," as she puts it. As I begin, Dharma ambles up with her powder puff puppy and sits beside Grace, protective and interested.

"She's talking about family," Grace explains my questions to Dharma, "which is a loaded topic for me."

"It's the opposite for me," Dharma laughs, and I'm surprised by the kids' interpretations of their respective backgrounds.

Grace openly jumps into her life story, her speech speedy. "There were three girls that were really close to me. They're my cousins, and we were all born in the same year. We're really close, and we grew up living together, so we're like sisters, even though we're cousins. One of them became a heroin addict when I was, like, fourteen, so I pretty much spent the past four years taking care of her, helping her. In the past year, I started dating this boy who I knew when I was really young. He was a heroin addict, so the past couple months for me have just been crazy chaotic, because I've been taking care of all these heroin addicts and taking care of my family members. My grandma died in February this year for essentially being an alcoholic."

Grace tells me she's come here, to Rainbowland, to escape Seattle, to take a break from the shitstorm that is her family life. "I've been super anxiety ridden since I've been down here... I've been worrying about them, even though I'm five states away from Washington."

The sky suddenly cracks into thunder, but Grace keeps talking, telling me about her past without reservation. I ask her how she hasn't become a drug addict herself, being surrounded by it since infancy.

"When I was fourteen, I did heroin. I did a lot of drugs. The first real drug I ever did, I was thirteen, and I smoked crack... I lost at least thirty friends in the decision to not do drugs. A lot of

A woman crowd-surfs ecstatically on the Fourth of July, supported by friends and newfound family.

NEW MEXICO, JULY 2009

them called me a narc afterwards, even though it's not like I was ratting on them... and I lost a handful of my family members by deciding I didn't want to do drugs anymore."

I am shocked by this statement. It makes me start to understand why kids would want to come to Rainbow for an alternative family structure. Grace tells me, however, that she's not that into Rainbow—that she's experienced sexual abuse here: jeers, comments, catcalls. She thinks she fits in much better with the punks and Schwilly kids.

"Maybe when I'm older I'll appreciate the whole vibe more, but since I've been down here, it's like, you *love me*? Fuck you! You don't even know me. That's how I feel. Like, '*Lovin' you*'? I'm like, fuck you! I'm not lovin' you. You don't even know who I am. Screw you! Tell me you love me when you get to know me!"

In the background, in the rain, Dharma's older sister, Emma, is wrestling in a newly formed mud pit beside the fire.

"Three, two, one, fight!"

Emma sloshes around, fully brown, covered from head to toe in dirt. She challenges a number of men twice her size to wrestle her and then beats every one without contest. It's like she's sending a message, and Grace's comments show me why she would want to. A gash of blood appears on Emma's arm, but she keeps fighting. Unlike her bubbly sister, she seems less idealistic, perhaps more weathered by the road. When she's finished fighting, she agrees to sit with me, away from the mud pit, and chat. First, she tells me about how she found Rainbowland.

"Well, I was homeless since I was thirteen and some guy kinda swooped up through town one day, and he was like, 'Come to a Rainbow Gathering with me. I'm going.' He wasn't, like, one of those brother-mother-lovers type of deals, whatever. He was a kids' kid, you know? He was a fucking hardcore kid. And he took me to a Rainbow Gathering, gave me two pounds of pot, and said, 'Figure it out.'"

"And did you figure it out?" I ask.

"Yeah. I figured a lot of things out. It was a really big eye-opener for me, actually. First, I was one of the really frilly dilly hippie-dippie kids. And then, you really... you can't end up trusting everybody—I learned the hard way."

I decide not to press her, sensing her unease. She stares out at the field.

"In the end, I still come to these things only because I get to see my kids, like, once a year. We are all traveling around and we never get to see each other unless we're in the same city, and it's a pain in the ass to catch up with each other. So it's kinda nice to get everyone in one spot and catch up with each other."

It seems this is a common story: the festival acts as a calm constant, filled with food and shelter and emotional support, to help many homeless kids and travelers network, heal, and feel safe somewhere. Rainbow often acts as a meeting point for travelers who have been moving all year, a place to come back to for a few days, or weeks, to catch up and calm down.

I ask Emma what she means when she says her "kids."

"Well, there's the people who come to Rainbow Gatherings, the ones that are nice and clean. You know they just come for the hippie stuff. Then there's the kids that have nowhere else to go, who have been coming to these things since they were babies— the kids that didn't have families. And we all show up and we are each other's family... I'm a kid. I'll be a kid until the day I die."

Next to the Dirty Kid campfire, Sicka, the scowling redhead, lifts her Misfits shirt to reveal a gash, four hands wide, across her gut. Unlike mainstream girls her age, she isn't self-conscious about her disheveled hair or puffy waistline: she has more important things to worry about.

"Got stabbed back in Portland," she tells me, almost apathetically, pulling the shirt back over her gash. "Almost died."

Sicka sucks on a morning smoke and passes it to a friend beside her. She says she had to carry her own guts in her hands to the hospital. I feel nauseous.

"I guess that's what you get for trying to save someone's life," she concludes, laughing menacingly. Sicka explains she was attacked when she tried to break up a fight between a fellow traveling kid and her abusive boyfriend. Sicka is no stranger to violence, having been surrounded by it since birth.

"When I was thirteen, I pressed charges on my stepmom and dad—child abuse. I have a twin sister. She has cerebral palsy. My stepmom would beat the shit out of her. I would get double the beatings so I wouldn't have to see her get hit. I was so traumatized from my childhood that I started drinking heavily and doing meth and coke, smoking crack, when I was thirteen years old. So by the time I turned fifteen, I was so fucked off in my head, I hated myself, and so I successfully killed myself for eighty-six seconds. It was, like, my fifth suicide attempt, but I successfully did it this time. So, they gave me 180 days."

Sicka was admitted to a mental institution and put on heavy medication for a laundry list of mental health diagnoses.

"Diag*nonsense* is more like it," she jokes. She is clear and eloquent, with quick eyes that are growing kinder.

"I don't talk to my dad anymore. I tried to call him recently. He actually broke up with my stepmom, thank god, and he's got a new girlfriend. I'm gay and he wants to impress his girlfriend. I don't think he wants to introduce me. He doesn't talk to me anymore. I kind of disowned him. He disowned me. Whatever."

These days, Sicka sells her meds and receives social assistance checks. She also occasionally makes money opening for rock bands as a freak show artist with shocking self-mutilation talents. She says she learned to stick needles through her cheeks and objects down her esophagus in the mental institution. It's also where she came out of the closet.

"There were a lot of cute girls in there." Sicka laughs as the sun goes down.

By nighttime, Kitra's camera battery is low. Electricity isn't always easily accessible in Rainbowland; many of the appliances are human powered, bike powered, vegetable oil powered. We trek up the hill to Bus Village, a camp consisting of nearly a hundred school buses and RVs, to see if anyone will let us use their electrical plug-in. A short man with round glasses seems eager to help. He leads us to his cherry-red pickup truck parked just a few yards away.

"Happy to help, sisters," he says, opening his car door. He asks us what we're up to out here, and we tell him we're a writer and photographer doing a story on Rainbowland.

"No kidding! I'm a writer, too," he says. "Actually, I write children's books." His mood shifts slightly. "I used to camp in Kiddie Village, actually, but I'm not allowed there anymore."

Kitra and I share a glance. Kiddie Village, I've been told, is the family camp, a place bursting with babies and inquisitive children, collective crafting, and New Age traveling families.

"Why not?" I venture.

"They said my books weren't appropriate for children."

The man pulls out a book from the back seat. It's printed on bright, glossy paper. The illustrations depict confused images of body parts: erections and nipples dancing awkwardly, cartoonishly, with childlike figures. The colors are horrible, soupy and psychedelic, and make me feel queasy.

"Well, ladies, here are the keys," the man says quickly, noting our lack of response. "Just leave them on top of the wheel when you're done."

After the man leaves, Kitra and I shift awkwardly in our seats as the battery recharges. I don't know what's worse: the sudden realization that we're in a cherry-red truck belonging to a potential child molester or the fact that we now have his keys and an opportunity to jack his vehicle.

In his ethnography, Michael Niman states: "Rainbows profess that the best place to start building a global peace is locally, by making Gatherings into models of peaceful coexistence and nonviolent conflict resolution. The Rainbow Family has its share, however, of child predators, rapists, muggers, and thieves. Members acknowledge that whatever's 'out there' in Babylon is also 'in here' at Gatherings. The Family is, after all, a microcosm of the greater society." Although I know this, I am still shocked by our encounter, and by the man's openness in discussing his experience.

An hour later, we walk back down the hill to our tents and never discuss the incident again. I attempt to get a good night's rest, but my mind keeps revisiting the colors, soupy and psychedelic, which leak into my subconscious like sewage.

RELAXING BY THE Dirty Kids fire pit the following day, I find a young woman dressed in salvaged fur. I suspect she is also new to the Rainbow scene, which I soon find to be true. When I ask to interview her, she obliges immediately.

Her name is Arianna and she speaks in a contemplative, dreamy voice. She's been traveling for two months straight, living in a big brown school bus, which recently broke down.

"I went to a Grateful Dead concert and never went home to Santa Cruz, because it felt right to go off with this random person I barely knew. I can't really explain it."

I ask her if Rainbow is her family now, and she laughs.

"That's interesting. 'Family': I don't really like that word because it means some people are your family and others are 'they,' or not your family. So it's sectioning off people. I don't really like to use that word . . . it separates."

Since starting to travel, Arianna says she has changed. "I've learned to open up a little bit more," she tells me. "Something that really helped me with that is not having a home base, 'cause what happens when people have a home—a house, I mean—is that they go out in the world and they kind of restrain themselves, and they, like, use their house to be themselves and to open up. And so constantly being around people and just constantly being traveling, you kind of have to learn to just have your house wherever you are."

Back at the tent, I think about the separation between home and travel, about my own lack of experience on the road. Kitra insists that we don't have to be outsiders, that this is our choice too, that we can live this life. She says these people can become our genuine friends, our new family. I tell her that we will never be insiders, that our cameras and recorders are tools of separation, machines that will always keep us separate. She continues to disagree.

ON THE FOURTH of July, I wake exhausted. We've been in Rainbowland for days now. Offensive scents penetrate the tent, assaulting my early-morning senses. I'm overwhelmed by the smells that hang in the air like stained sheets: patchouli oil and peppery sage, dog piss and burnt pines, and the unlimited fonts of vile body odor. In Rainbowland, you can't escape the reek of the living. Kitra and I lie together in our tent, puffy eyed. I notice she's beginning to grow a film of dirt on her pale white skin; her face looks like a dirty nickel.

"We should go to Main Meadow today," she says. "We need to shoot some more portraits."

For Kitra, the barrier between work and life is ever indistinguishable; she seems fueled by this.

I nod. I brush my teeth and chug a jar of iced coffee (I'd insisted we buy some at the Walmart in Albuquerque, and now I'm running dangerously low). I eye her lips greedily as she takes a small sip. Today is the official day of the Prayer for Peace. Beyond my preliminary research, I'm unsure what this prayer entails, or how exactly to participate, but simply know it is the central event of this Rainbow Gathering. I snatch back my coffee, and Kitra and I resume discussing our plan of action. As if on cue, a stranger's claw shoves under our tent door, handing us a note: *TODAY IS THE PRAYER FOR PEACE—PLEASE OBSERVE SILENCE* ☺.

We immediately stifle flabbergasted giggles. Kitra grabs the note and scrawls an apologetic "Thanks!" on the back, returning it under the door.

Silently, we grab our gear and head down to Main Meadow, where the field is bustling with bodies. Rainbows have arrived in swaths and the open land is peppered with toothy grins. Folks are streaming in from the path. Many of the new arrivals look clean-cut, wearing white dashikis, prayer beads, and expensive sunglasses. These participants usually spend only a few days at the Gathering and are often referred to as weekend warriors. This label comes with mixed connotations. Weekend warriors, also known as wws, are considered Family but not nomads. They often have nine-to-five jobs and live primarily in Babylon. Even though their daily Babylonian life stands in opposition to Rainbow culture, they come bearing valuable gifts—sacks of sweet potatoes, bunches of kale, pasta, rice—and so they are welcome. They also offer monetary donations for the Magic Hat, an anonymous communal money pool used to fund the event and buy supplies—medicine, hardware, and sustenance—for everyone on-site. Few wws stick around for the weeks of cleanup, go on dumpster runs, lead kitchens, or get deeply embedded in longer-term Rainbow culture. This causes a rift with many full-time Rainbow folks, who often attend Gatherings out of necessity, not just for pleasure.

Although full-time Rainbows appreciate the gifts wws bring, they could get along without them. In his ethnography, Michael Niman notes that the funds raised through passing the hat are minimal, giving the approximate amount of money raised for the 1990 Minnesota Gathering at $4,000, which would be closer to $7,500 in 2016. Contrast that with the $310,000 spent that summer by the U.S. National Forest Service to monitor and patrol that particular event, or the $573,361 spent in 2013 by law enforcement and forest services to monitor the Gathering. This is a testament to the resourcefulness and open sharing practices of participants, who run large-scale events on little money, as well as an example of the exorbitant amount of taxpayer money local authorities dish out annually in an attempt to control the event.

By midday, the swarms at Main Meadow have arranged themselves in a number of perfect concentric circles. Everyone holds hands. On the periphery of the field, a fleet of about twenty or so cops and rangers are dressed in green uniforms and stacked atop black, speckled horses. They watch the festivities with confused titillation. Some Rainbows smile and engage them, offering hugs or flowers or handshakes. Most Rainbows ignore their presence completely.

"Seven up!" snarls a dreadlocked Rainbow defiantly in the direction of the group.

Anxiously, I nudge my way into a ring of new faces, losing Kitra in the bustle. In the center of the circle stand a number of elders, including an older woman in a long white gown. The woman silences the crowd of thousands with a single finger to her lips. I don't know who she is, but I look to her for direction, sensing she knows what's going on. Nervous coughs and tics surface then fade, and the silence starts. Friends and family members, young and old, nomadic and Babylonian, hold hands, eyes closed, feet planted on the earth. Thousands of still citizens (there are more than twenty thousand of us, I later learn) stand assembled away from buildings, stadiums, or squares—in nature. The silent crowd is astounding. A single person starts to chant "Om," and the call catches on. A collective hum, slow at first, gains steam. "Om."

I don't want to let it in. I resist, confused about what we're actually "doing" here, chuckling to myself at how silly this whole thing seems. I long to remain an observer. I am, after all, on assignment, I think, and should attempt to remain objective, detached, outside. Yet, after some time, the noise nudges its way in. It enters slowly, through my skin, past my common sense, into me entirely. My mouth opens on its own, and I start to make noise without realizing it, subtle at first, then more forceful. The om-ing turns to humming, a sheet of loose human noise. I sink into the sound of the bodies surrounding me—naked, clothed, breathing, stinking—under the sky. I inhale the aroma of smoke and sweat and sweet grass and hold on tighter to the strangers' hands beside me. I close my eyes and let my head fall back in release. The humming turns to screaming, laughing, a maniacal shriek of human existence! Joy, terror, extremity, all together, all at once, overarching, everywhere! The unity arrives, and I'm nobody to question it. I can feel it in every faculty, all along my unwashed skin, up my spine, and over my crust-filled eyes. Human ecstasy! The sky cracks open, happy with us, and down comes the rain. Pouring, surging, nonsensical! Random, welcome wetness! Humans release hands and bodies begin to dance, to move and shift and squirm, euphoric. My mouth is filled with water. Young and old women toss their clothes on the ground and run naked through the meadow. I hear the drums, the bongos, the djembes, the yelps and squeals of a crowd on fire. Suddenly, a cart of ripe green watermelons materializes and the fruit is slashed and distributed to the crowd. I'm offered a pink piece of melon and I suckle on the juices, devour the fruit fully. A child wearing a panda suit sucks on a green rind beside me, giggling. I'm filthy, wet, and wild-eyed, terrified beyond comprehension, and I can't stop laughing. I feel more joy than I have ever felt before.

As the day continues, the rain makes a mud pit and a hundred people dance inside it, their bodies covered with thick brown mud. Teens and old folks roll around in mud puddles, and a few begin crowd surfing on the backs of others. Their body heat causes a great mist, a nimbus of sweat and condensation. Drums create a ring around the pit and a loose beat guides the muddy stomping. In a flashback to my studies at McGill, I'm reminded of the Asaro Mudmen, the Papua New Guinea tribe who covered their bodies in river mud to scare off invaders. I think how terrified people back home would be if they could see this scene, wonder if the onlooking cops are afraid. This thought excites me. I enter the mud pit, allowing one of the dancers to give me a sloppy full-body mud hug. A huge nude red-haired woman approaches me and begins roping me into her dance, bulbous breasts bouncing, covered in mud. I see all the folds of her flesh, her rippling belly, her alive eyes. People cry in one another's arms all around, and I'm astounded, overwhelmed. Despite all my protestations, all my longing to stay outside of this experience, I feel, for a split second, like I am part of something. I feel like I'm home.

After the Prayer for Peace, the skies clear and Kitra ambles up to me through the crowd of thousands. I wonder how she's found me. She says she had been perched on the periphery, snapping photos the whole time.

"Wow," I say.

She smiles calmly, then snaps a photo of me in that moment.

CHAPTER 2

Food Stamps in Babylon

(JULY 2009)

THE NEXT DAY we're heading to Babylon, stocking up on foodstuffs and supplies mid-Rainbow. This is a regular task—people come and go from the festival often—but returning to Babylon during a Gathering is daunting. You never seem to fit in the same way.

We drive to Mickey Save-Way Market in Moe's busted up Jeep: Sal; Josh; Sicka and her girlfriend, Moe; two kids named Thaddeus and Frankie; as well as Dapper Dan the doggy and two other salivating pups whose names I don't know. Kitra and I hold on for dear life. The car is packed with kids and stinks like shit. The dirty kids need junk food: cookies, peanut butter, and Kraft Dinner, and they have a monthly allotment of food stamps. They have enough assistance to feed themselves all month, but stamps don't pay for pot or booze. Inside, the storeowners suspect we're stealing, and some of the Rainbows are, but not Josh. He's just standing there, barefoot, salivating at a package of frozen sausages. He wears a knee-length, frilly blue gown and his hairy legs jut out like caterpillars.

"Got this sexy number a few towns back," he tells me. "Now all the girls won't stop trying to trade me for it."

Josh decides the sausages are too steep for his budget. He saunters up to the till and grabs a candy bar, handing the cashier a grubby food stamp card, which she takes hesitantly. Josh doesn't seem to notice he's cross-dressing in a hyper-conservative Podunk town—or he doesn't care. His card is declined and we are asked to leave the store.

A middle-aged Rainbow woman with three grubby babies begs for food outside the entrance. Signs promoting deals and ideas fight for space on the store's bib: *United We Stand, Fireworks and Chicken for Sale.* Company slogans scream in pink and yellow: *Doritos, Taquitos, Tostitos, Spam.* Other Rainbow teens sit outside "spanging": asking for spare change with homemade signs crafted from discarded beer boxes. This practice, common to many broke travelers, includes "flying a sign" on the sidewalk or creatively asking for money somehow. Many travelers and tramps live hand to mouth, on only the money they are able to wrangle that day, or no money at all. Other travelers, commonly known as "trustafarians," live off their trust funds and family wealth (though many do not advertise this openly).

Frankie sits beside the jeep, poking at a can of refried beans with her jackknife. Moe and Sicka make out, their breasts bumping against each other as townies in cowboy hats stare with mouths agape. The puppies lick at stray puddles.

"How are y'all doing?" A group of clean Bible-carrying Christians approach our vehicle. "We would sure love to help you guys out," they say, handing out protein bars with helpline numbers on the back.

Since I was raised by atheists, I feel an ingrained pang of suspicion. What do they want from us? They tell us they run a nearby shelter, where we are always welcome.

"We've even got some dog food for your pups!" a man in a

white cowboy hat says, pointing at Dapper Dan. The dirty kids respond warmly.

"Hey, thanks, man," Thaddeus says, snagging a bar. "I love Christians," he concludes before taking a bite.

It might seem like straitlaced Christians and dirty, bohemian Rainbows wouldn't get along, but the Christians do seem to be the only Babylonians not gawking or shouting things at us from their car windows. Their attention also comes with the bonus of free food.

After groceries, we stop at a Shell station to "gas can"—beg for dregs of gas from patrons already pumping. Sal grabs a red container from the trunk and begins his rounds. This is a common practice among young travelers and an almost surefire way to get where you're going—that is, if you have a car. Gas-pumping patrons can give in a way that makes them feel comfortable, knowing their contribution isn't going to drugs or booze but directly into the tank.

The inside of Moe's car is lined with cardboard signs, many of which are misspelled: *Travlin' and Broke Down*, *Hungry & Heading South*, *Need Ga$*. The walls of the truck are covered with tags from all the kids who've ridden in it, hieroglyphs of adventures past.

After half an hour, tired of waiting around, Kitra and I kick down a twenty for gas, charging it to the magazine's bill. We fill the tank, load the truck, and head out to a nearby hot spring before the sun goes down. We want to keep following this accepting crew, taking their photos and interviewing them.

Once we get to the spring, the mood gets loose.

"Don't you dare call me a faggot!" Sal screams at nobody in particular. He's drunk and naked, clutching a bottle of root beer in one hand and a jug of Jack Daniel's in the other. "I'm *queer*," he says indignantly, sitting down on Josh's bare lap. "It's *different*."

I will learn that an overwhelming majority of the homeless teens or performers on the road identify as queer, gay, trans, or

LGBTQ2. Many have taken to the road because they have been kicked out of their homes or alienated because of their identity. I find Rainbow's open atmosphere comforting, being queer identified myself and having felt alienated within both my own family and community as a result. Straightness is not assumed in Rainbowland, nor is it deemed supreme.

The spring, at first shockingly warm, soothes my sunburns and bug bites. Kitra and I are naked and submerged. Mud and sludge melt off of us like hot butter. We watch the shenanigans from the sidelines. Sal's yelps unnerve the more demure Babylonian bathers sharing the hot spring, who eye us suspiciously. In Babylon, the kids can drink excessively and out in the open without breaking the Rainbow rule against booze, and they are taking full advantage of this luxury.

"I heard that salt water heals scabies!" Moe jokes, hoping to clear the crowded spring and make more room for her friends.

"What about herpes?" Josh kids.

"Or hep C?"

It works. Strangers' bodies exit the spring quickly: they don't want to chance infection.

Soon, we're alone. In the water, kids compare bites and cuts, nipples and scars, their mouths slurping whiskey and swapping spit with their friends and lovers. I forget who's dating whom, but it doesn't matter anymore. The boundaries of young bodies blur under hot water. I'm introduced to a whole cast of tattoos: barbed wire, peace signs, and stick-and-poke tattoos done with just a needle and ink aplenty. I am surrounded by exposed skin. But nobody stares or points. Nobody criticizes. The kids are confident with their bodies, a somewhat strange phenomenon, I note, for North American teenagers. They willingly let Kitra snap nude photos. I try my best to keep out of the frame.

"Come on, Dan, jump in!" Sal shouts, and his puppy bounds fearlessly into the spring. A membrane of fur unfolds atop the water. "Good boy!"

When the night begins to cool, Moe and Sicka are still necking. They're clean now, dirt stripped off. Their soft bodies come together like folded hands. Moe breaks off suddenly, jumping atop a rock, proudly displaying her lean, perfect frame: I admire her thinness, her round breasts and moonlit skin. I admire her ability to expose herself so openly, without reservation. Sicka's stomach looms underwater. I can see the outline of the stab wound from across the spring. A black tattoo under her neck reads *Tilt*. She exhales smoke through her teeth as her girlfriend shouts and drinks. Sicka licks her chapped lips in the murky water as the daylight vanishes into darkness.

Panic hits me. I realize the hike out, without a flashlight, will be nearly impossible. It took us an hour to climb up here in broad daylight, and I have no sweater, no towel, and no sober ride back to Rainbow. As usual, Kitra is unfazed, soaking up her surroundings, constantly clicking. I tell her I'm tired. She nods. She is ready to spend the night with these kids, ready to wake up in the morning and do it all over again, every day, from here on out. She seems annoyed when she realizes I want to leave. I convince a stranger with a flashlight and a car to take me back to the Gathering, and Kitra comes with me, grudgingly.

THE FIRST TIME I went to Kitra's home in Montreal, I wept. I hadn't experienced a family like hers before, and it was overwhelming. She got along with her four siblings and seemed genuinely happy to live at home. She was in utter awe of her father, a rabbi-poet. It was at Shabbat dinner that night that he told us something I couldn't forget.

"It's in the desert where God reveals himself," he said. He asked if anyone knew why, but nobody did. "In the desert there are no distractions."

I cried in the bathroom after that meal, ashamed of my response, my lack of spiritual knowledge. That night I saw God everywhere, even if he wasn't my own.

Sal and Sicka skinny-dip in a Babylonian hot spring. "Babylon" is the catchall term for everything outside of Rainbowland.

NEW MEXICO, JULY 2009

When we get back to Rainbow two hours later, there is a prophet standing in front of the Turtle Soup campfire, completely naked. The blond figure has breasts and a penis, human parts illuminated by rapturous flame, and they are preaching to an audience of rapt Rainbows, who are hanging off their every word.

"We are the Rainbow Warriors," the nude prophet orates. "We are the followers of the white buffalo... we chant to our ancient ancestors. We chant to Krishna, to Vishnu, to Jesus, to Gandhi." The individual shifts in the darkness. Rapt eyes follow.

Open Vision Counsels are held near the end of each Gathering to determine the region and spot of the next Gathering, and it seems one is happening outside our tent.

"Two thousand years ago, white calf buffalo women came to the tribes. After Atlantis sunk under, white people were sent to the North to be keepers of the knowledge of the fire. The black to the South to be keepers of the rhythm. The yellow people to the East to be keepers of the knowledge of the breath and the red people to the West to be keepers of the knowledge of the earth."

I don't know how to process this information, so I simply record it.

A common criticism of the Family is their frequent appropriation of cultural practices, customs, and dress, particularly that of Indigenous peoples. Sacred feathers, loincloths, and dream catchers abound, though the absence of actual Indigenous attendees is obvious and notable. It is mainly white folks who are erecting these teepees and leading sweats. It is troubling to observe, to say the least.

In *People of the Rainbow*, Niman mentions that many Rainbows see themselves as the reincarnation of Indigenous tribes and people, most popularly the Hopi. Indigenous activist Andrea Smith comments on this aptly in Niman's ethnography: "[Rainbows] want to become Indian without holding themselves accountable to Indian communities. If they did, they would have to listen to Indians telling them to stop carrying around sacred pipes, stop doing their sweat lodges, and stop appropriating our spiritual practices. Rather these New Agers see Indians as romanticized gurus who exist only to meet their consumerist needs."

I have witnessed this appropriation constantly throughout my stay in Rainbowland, especially in the more "New Age" or "hippie" camps. But since I'm here to interview teenage runaways, most of whom camp with punks who wouldn't be caught dead wearing sacred feathers or practicing any "spiritual" activity, I haven't had to face this firsthand—until now. The figure at the fire continues their oration:

"The Tibetans and the Hopi speak the same language, and some of their words are flipped backwards. We have come back together: it has nothing to do with the economy. It is the first time in history. And this is what it's about—it's about moving forward. We've got the histories, we've learned the lessons, and now it's time to take a step in the next direction."

The prophet stands in the summer darkness, their speech finished. No consensus is reached on the location of the next Gathering, but everyone seems satisfied for now. After the crowd dissipates, I fall back into my tent, exhausted. Smells of chai and chocolate seep through my plastic tent as I fall asleep on the forest floor.

Like all Rainbows, this one eventually ends. When I wake up the next morning, people are already beginning to leave. I am told the kitchens will be disassembled and packed. The hippies will go home and the nomads will hit the road. Many road kids and hobos will stay on the grounds for a few weeks to convert the wilderness back to its original state—but at this point, I need to go back to Canada.

Before I leave, I make one last stop at Dirty Kids Camp. Many of the kids are lounging, drinking whiskey, and catching up on lost sleep. Few attended the Prayer for Peace the day before, opting to hang out back at camp and get drunk. I exchange contact information with some of the people I've interviewed and plan when to meet up next. Kids swap cell phone numbers, emails, and online contacts; many travelers use free Internet at fast-food chains, libraries, or coffee shops to keep in touch.

Pop bottles and tarps lie willy-nilly on the mud, and it's hard to imagine this meadow will ever be returned to its pristine condition. Kids might be sad about leaving, but nobody complains. There's talk of Ocala, Florida, of regional Gatherings, of farms and squats. As the night creeps in, the teens circle the Dirty Kids campfire one last time, singing, screaming, sitting too close to the flames. Rain begins to fall again, but no one takes notice. The fire lights human and canine faces alike. As dogs yelp and hump, the dirty kids find comfort picking their ticks, nursing sunburns and scars, huddled together for warmth.

CHAPTER 3

⁗⁗⁗⁗⁗⁗⁗⁗⁗⁗⁗⁗⁗

Nomadia

(AUGUST 2009)

"**H**ARE KRISHNA HARE Krishna, Krishna Krishna Hare Hare."

It's morning and the Hare Krishnas are chanting outside our tent. My best friend, Terra, and I are camped out at Sacred Spaces, one of the many camps on the barren playa landscape. I'm at the Burning Man festival. The Krishnas control our kitchen.

"Hare Krishna Hare Krishna, Krishna Krishna Hare Hare."

"I'm getting really fucking sick of this song," Terra yells sharply through our dust-covered tent. She's wearing huge industrial goggles and a button-up shirt tucked into clean white panties. She sucks on a puffer between angered exclamations; the playa dust is aggravating her asthma. "Enough already! I mean, at first it was cool, but now it's like *get some new material*!"

It's the end of the summer and I'm taking a vacation before school starts. I've decided to return to the middle of the Nevada desert to write about another quirky subset of American nomadic culture: the burner. It's my second time at Burning Man in two years, and I'm high off the fumes of last month's Rainbow. I'm feeling light, looking to learn more about the nomadic life, to connect with others and sink into movement more completely.

Black Rock City, the name bestowed upon this temporary settlement, is a fully functional metropolis that is built seemingly overnight on the desolate alkaline flats way north of Reno, Nevada. Every summer, upward of fifty thousand freaks head into the Nevada dessert to regroup and unplug. But Burning Man hasn't always been big: the first event was held in 1986, my birth year, with a beach bonfire in San Francisco. The festival eventually moved out into the desert as numbers, and interest, grew. The human horde builds infrastructure and art installations, huffs inhalants, dances hedonistically, and tries to hear God. Black Rock City comes with streets, sanitation, Porta Potties, neon lights, and an unparalleled, almost incomprehensible amount of absolute absurdity. In the end—and there is a very definitive beginning and end to this festival—the iconic wooden man that sits at the center of Black Rock City is burnt to the ground, and most burners, who are seldom full-time travelers themselves (though some are), go back to their homes, lives, and nine-to-five or part-time jobs.

I'm curious to know how this subset of nomad lives and plays, how a more middle-class event with a price tag compares to the free, all-access Rainbowland. I want to know if Rainbows and burners are entirely different species or if there is some interplay between the two groups.

Last year, Terra and I camped with Green Tortoise Camp from San Francisco. They provided bus services into the festival and all our food. Since we were coming from outside the country, this made the most sense to us, despite the $700 price tag for ticket, transport, camping, and meal plan. We have been told the Krishnas serve delicious vegan food, and despite our limited student budgets, we decided to spring for the luxury. The fee is $128 for camping and then an additional $211 for the meal plan.

Like last year, we applied for low-income tickets, which are made available for artists and students. We received these discounted tickets, which ran us $190, only after proving our destitute state with written confessionals and bank statements.

"Hare Krishna Hare Krishna, Krishna Krishna Hare Hare."

Outside, the men continue their chant ceaselessly.

AT BLACK ROCK CITY, bass is omnipresent. This year there are more than 43,000 attendees (the number swelled to 70,000 in 2016). Unlike at Rainbow, where human hands produce all music (a process some call "organic music"), burners prefer electronic beats. As I exit my tent, I spot the entrance for a camp called Burning Tran, a huge complex marked at the doorway by an armless mannequin, complete with plastic breasts and large plastic penis. I spy three topless women sitting in a large crown, kissing and taking selfies. We chat and I take their photo. Down the street from Burning Tran is Spank Camp, where volunteers line up to be whacked in the butt by a homemade ass-paddling machine.

There are obvious and significant differences between Rainbowland and Burning Man: Rainbow is held in a different national forest every year; Burning Man is always held in the dry, rough belly of the Nevada desert. Rainbowland is entirely devoid of technology, whereas Burning Man is built upon it, almost in homage to it, really. Rainbow is virtually unknown by mainstream culture, whereas Burning Man is well known, referenced jokingly on shows as popular as *The Simpsons*.

The main difference between the two festivals is class-based: Burning Man has a gate and you must purchase a ticket, whereas access to Rainbowland is entirely free. The burner occupies a different financial bracket than the Rainbow. Low-income tickets to Burning Man are readily available for those struggling financially, but many travelers view the festival as a more economically privileged "yuppie" scene. On the one hand, most burners can afford to spend close to four hundred dollars on a festival ticket and hundreds of bucks on an organic, raw, or vegan meal plan, not to mention the plane ticket to get there in the first place. Although the high price of admission is sometimes criticized, much of the funds go to finance the impressive and expansive infrastructure, art installations, sanitation, security, emergency first aid, and overall operation of the festival. On the other, many Rainbows are penniless, arriving at festivals on foot, by hopped train, or by hitched ride.

Despite this considerable difference, there are similarities, too. Both festivals are transient spaces, and both function on a gifting or trade economy (the only things you can buy at Burning Man are ice and coffee at Center Camp, a large structure in the center of the city full of resting benches, healers, tarot card readers, and acrobatic equipment). Like Rainbows, burners have a "leave no trace" mentality, spending a large amount of ticket sales revenue to ensure the festival is properly cleaned up afterwards (though a good deal of burners are straight-up hedonists, hell-bent on destruction). Burners and Rainbows share a love for communal living, an interest in impermanent settlements, and a general opposition to straight, consumerist culture (as an example of the sharing culture burners create, my old roommate once went to Burning Man without a ticket and waited at the front gate until a middle-aged woman in a convertible arrived and gave away five free tickets to bystanders). Both events embody examples of the possibilities outside of our current static, consumerist culture. And both festivals attract tens of thousands of nomadic nutbars like moths to a flame, myself included.

Whenever I leave my tent on this trip, my senses are assaulted by strange scenes all around me. Nude couples bike by, holding hands, swerving with intoxicated laughter. In the distance, passersby ride a twelve-foot-tall seesaw for free, provided the riders are topless. Men call down from the seesaw, luring possible

participants, while women bounce up and down, laughing shame-
lessly, breasts jiggling. As I reach Center Camp, I watch art cars
zip past—vehicles transformed into art pieces. There is a prayer
temple built of white wood, accessible by bike, foot, or hopped
art car (hitchhiking on the playa is commonplace). At the temple,
which will eventually be burnt to the ground, participants are
invited to engrave on the walls the names of loved ones who have
passed, and to construct personal shrines to say good-bye. Terra
leaves a note for her father, who passed when she was young.
I can't even see the city limits; the scale of Black Rock City is
almost unbelievable. I feel small, insane, and awestruck.

In an article for Mashable, Chris Taylor describes the kind of
people who thrive in the playa environment: "People who are a
little bit crazy, quite a bit determined, and a whole lot of wiry and
smart. People with an Iggy Pop–style lust for life. Here are punks
of all stripes: cyberpunks, steampunks, biker punks, *punk* punks.
People who do what it says on the ticket—voluntarily assume the
risk of death." I agree with this statement—with a caveat: Burning Man is for punks with money.

Much like Rainbow, a festival as big as Burning Man
needs some rules. Here, too, there's no one leader—though the
co-founder of the festival, Larry Harvey, wrote out the Ten Principles of the festival in 2004. These guiding principles are posted
throughout the playa, as well as on the Internet. The rules, which
range from radical inclusion of strangers from all walks of life
to radical self-reliance, meaning each individual is responsible
for their own water, food, shelter, and personal safety, all place
an emphasis on personal accountability and mutual respect for
fellow freaks. The final rule, "Immediacy," is a bit more con-
ceptual. It reads: "Immediate experience is, in many ways, the
most important touchstone of value in our culture. We seek to
overcome barriers that stand between us and a recognition of
our inner selves, the reality of those around us, participation in

society, and contact with a natural world exceeding human powers. No idea can substitute for this experience."

Despite the playa rules, there is a notably less environmentally friendly vibe in this crowd compared to Rainbowland. After all, burners have an insatiable thirst for fire. Burners constantly burn shit. At night, neon-lit school buses slouch down the dusty streets shooting fireworks. Huge flamethrowers sit atop six-foot-tall moving structures. There is a replica of New York's Wall Street, which will eventually burn to the ground, black smoke billowing. People are burnt, broken, and some die. That evening, standing on a tall scaffold, blasting a flamethrower forward into the Nevada night, I feel very comfortable. People here live outwardly, honestly. I'm drawn to the extremity, the open chaos, the wild flame. Wearing a top hat, I traverse the playa on foot, shoes coated in a thick layer of sludge.

SHE LOOKS NOTHING like my mother, but she's old enough to be. My shaking hands grasp sunburnt flesh; silicone pouches bounce back beneath my terrified fingertips. I just met Suzanne ten minutes ago and now I'm rubbing her sweaty nipples like a kid popping pimples on their friend's back. My mother would not approve.

I've landed, by a clumsy accident, in an intimate massage seminar: a women-only hour-long class on how to give and receive sensual touch. Walking from the nearby Krishna food tent, hungover, I stumbled into the yurt hearing something about "woman" and "massage" and not thinking much further. Now, there are twenty women, forty thighs, and twenty tongues, and we are all (mandatorily) topless.

Just breathe, I think. *Stay calm. You've got this.*

Women lie in pairs across the yurt, nipples in staring contests, a landscape of lady and woman and girl. A floral towel has been nailed to the entranceway to ensure privacy. It has also, I notice,

Burners clad in goggles and umbrellas experience the familiar menace of an impending Burning Man dust storm.

BLACK ROCK CITY, NEVADA, AUGUST 2009

closed off any chance of a discreet exit. I'm trapped, like a tick in a jar. The fear rises in the pit of my gut.

"Psst," Suzanne whispers, and I loosen what I suddenly realize is a firm grasp on her sticky breasts. The naked stranger shifts patiently.

"Is everything okay?" I ask.

"Yeah," she says.

"What's wrong?"

Suzanne stares into my wide eyes; she's pleading, aching, sad.

"Do you know what it's like to lose your soul mate?" she says.

I am caught off guard. I'm a child running in high-heeled shoes.

I'm twenty-two, I think. *What do I know about soul mates? I don't know shit about soul mates. I don't know shit about anything. And I certainly don't know shit about groping the tits of a grieving middle-aged woman in the middle of the Nevada desert!*

But Suzanne is looking at me like I'm an adult and she expects some sort of adult answer. I nod vigorously, not because I actually understand, but because I don't know what else to do with my head.

"Feel your partner's skin, intuit what she needs," the woman leading the seminar says from across the yurt. "Be here."

I am here and I am terrified.

An Everest of aging skin lies across the yurt from Suzanne and me, rearing high above the collage of other body parts. I shouldn't be looking over there—I should be concentrating on Suzanne, on her wants and needs—but it's hard not to stare. The mountainous woman is in her sixties and completely naked, though many of us have kept some clothes on. The boundaries of her body are blurry, as if drawn by a toddler: heaps of pearly-white thigh flesh, olive veins, a thorn bush of graying pubic hair. She has been partnered with a girl about my age, who sports long, rusty dreadlocks. The girl seems calm, almost placid, around her older partner. I watch as she puts her hands inside the woman, wading through her, stirring up musty smells and sound. In my head, I want to support this brave sisterly communion, but all I can see is something huge and gelatinous and dying and it makes me uncomfortable, so I look away.

Suzanne's eyes are beginning to tear up as the instructor tells us to slowly move down our partner's body. I rub my hands along her abdominal muscles, down her sides, past what I perceive as her age-inappropriate belly button piercing. Crying, Suzanne takes off her purple thong underwear and places it on the ground, beside her pair of folded purple fairy wings. I wonder who has seen her body since she lost her partner, if I am the first one. I see her razor burn, her birthmarks, her stretch marks, her pores and freckles. She smells like human dew.

"The tumor in his stomach made him hunch over," she says, in a daze. "I would wear nothing but six-inch heels, just so he would have to straighten up to kiss me."

I want to hold Suzanne tightly, to touch her effectively, to assure her she will find love again, that she will feel full again, that she will discover home and shelter and liveliness again, but I don't know if it's true, because I'm only twenty-two and I don't know anything. I wish Kitra was here to help me, at least to take pictures, to be a witness. I think back to the large red-haired woman I danced with in the Nevada forest, to the feeling of release we experienced together in the wild. I'm aching for that release, but it doesn't feel possible now.

"Keep rubbing," Suzanne says. "Just keep rubbing."

Across from us, Everest is beginning to climax. Her grunts and groans are like volcano burps, obnoxious, amphibian, slow at first, then more regular, louder, inevitable. I focus on Suzanne: middle-aged, beautiful, intact—part plastic but mostly real. Her lashes like little moths, fluttering: pupils playing hide-and-seek with the ceiling, eyes falling back into her head. The old mountain comes, a cough of ecstasy from across the yurt. Suzanne begins humming. *Suzanne, Suzanne, Suzanne.* There is no end, no climax, no peak, just Suzanne's soft humming. I focus on the hum. I put a hand on her chest. I keep rubbing.

AFTER THE DIVINE WOMAN workshop ends, I exit the yurt and walk onto the dusty playa, feeling shaken. Thousands of brightly dressed bodies and bikes lurch around the vast expanse of desert, alone, in pairs, atop double-decker buses shaped like Playboy bunnies. It is a Daliesque wonderland for the senses: a sensory overload. I've come here to study nomads, but most attendees I speak with are wealthy hedonists with major issues. Feeling overwhelmed, I head back to my campsite.

The weather changes without warning, and a dust storm forms. Clay and dirt whirlwinds; I can't see my own feet in front of me. As I stumble for shelter, coughing, a tall, thin figure emerges from the overarching gray. She smiles, shrugs her shoulders, and opens her arms to embrace me. *Am I hallucinating?*

"Kitra?"

"Hi!" the mirage says.

"What are you doing here?" I ask.

"I'm on assignment."

We are both a pile of questions and exclamation marks. She tells me she is here for *National Geographic*, covering the festival last-minute, all expenses paid. Her camera is wrapped in a plastic bag to shield it from the omnipresent dust. It's only been a few weeks since Rainbowland, but I've missed her greatly.

"I've been trying to find you," she says. "I'm doing a story on water. Have you seen any?"

At Burning Man, water is a big deal: all water must be brought in and out, and none can hit the playa floor. That is a real rule: no water on the playa floor—ever. At camps like Sacred Spaces, services come at a high cost, in part because they offer environmentally friendly shower bags, which allow a person to shower without dropping water, as well as meals. Regardless of this luxury, I remain dirty and dust covered for the entire festival. As stated in the rules, burners are expected to be radically self-reliant, meaning they must take care to bring in all their own supplies and entertainment, hydrate, and not burden anyone else, so these catered camps are often looked down upon by seasoned burners. Like Drainbows, many burners who rely on prepaid kitchens, such as Sacred Spaces or Green Tortoise, are seen as inferior to those who bring in all their own supplies.

Kitra and I make plans to meet up later, and I walk back to the Krishna camp perplexed and delighted.

"OH, COME ON!" Terra shouts from the top of the Thunderdome as two fighters attached to bungee cords bounce up and down on the ground below.

It's dusk and she's dressed in a skintight silver bodysuit and bright-purple wig. I sip on a mini bottle of wine beside her, wearing a top hat and a cheetah onesie, fifty feet off the ground. We are at one of my favorite attractions at Burning Man. The metal cage is a large-scale replica from the film *Mad Max Beyond Thunderdome*, where burners whack each other with padded sticks while heavy metal music blares and onlookers gawk and shout.

This would never happen in Rainbowland, I think to myself, watching the voluntary violence unravel beneath me, hanging onto the cage for dear life, laughing maniacally. I'm enlivened by the riffs and bass, drunk and frothing, delirious. I feel a sense of dangerous freedom. I am a little out of control. There is something about the outright tacky and unapologetic expression that appeals to me on a deep level. Folks are free to be freaks from start to finish of the festival. From this height, I can only see a fraction of the thriving Black Rock metropolis. I scan the endless neon sea, which extends into the desert unceasingly. In the distance, a white flag flies, alone and unclaimed. The flapping flag reads *Nomadia*. Beside it, a man wearing a fuzzy green thong exits a Porta Potty and picks his butt in the evening heat.

Home? I wonder. *Could I be home?*

CHAPTER 4

Cover Your Shit

(JULY 2010)

IT'S FOUR IN the morning and we're on the Upper East Side of Manhattan with our backpacks bulging. There's a gang of Hasidic Jews waiting for us in a black stretch van outside. We're crashing at Kitra's sister's sublet before returning to Rainbowland for the first time since last summer. It's been ten months since our last Rainbow and nine months since Burning Man. During the time in between, I returned to Vancouver for school and Kitra left for Belarus, to photograph and volunteer with the Jewish community there. Now we are headed to a Gathering in Pennsylvania. The men with the van have foot-long beards, pressed white shirts, pristine yarmulkes, and tzitzit, four prayer tassels hanging from under their shirts. I don't know how Kitra found them—she mentioned she met one of them on assignment in Belarus—but I've found it's best not to ask too many questions, just to trust her. Kitra introduces me as Christine, the *t* hanging in the air like a born-again crucifix.

"Morning, Family!" I try, optimistic in the early-morning air.

I'm greeted with an impenetrable wall of silence. Kitra tells me, discreetly, that it's these men's first Gathering. They aren't

Rainbows, they're ex-Hasidic Jews, and they have no idea what I'm talking about. It's a chilly morning and I become suddenly aware of my braless, erect nipples. The men avoid eye contact and remain silent; none offers his name in exchange.

"It is time to go," the driver announces, grabbing our bags and shoving them into the trunk.

I jump in the back with Kitra and slouch against the soft leather seating. A widescreen TV plays children's movies on a loop as the car revs and we hit the road.

"What's up with them?" I whisper to Kitra.

She shushes me. "They won't make us pay for gas."

I lie back and watch the movie, drifting off for a couple of hours. When I wake next we're at a gas station near the New York State border, filling up on junk food and fuel. The men seem more excited. The driver plays with a toy on the gas station shelf, a stuffed grandpa figurine that sings, "Don't you wish your grandpa was hot like me" when you push a button on his plush stomach. The low laughter of the men is soothing.

Next stop before Rainbow is, unfortunately, Walmart. Although I'm politically opposed to shopping here, it's become clear that many Rainbows inevitably stock up at Walmart before a Gathering because of the convenience and cheap prices. We are more prepared this time; we know which foods make good staples. We stockpile granola bars, hummus, and peanut butter. A line of merchandise called Faded Glory hangs on the Walmart racks, featuring images of tarnished American flags. I buy a travel pillow with a faded flag on the front. Surly Americans pass us in the aisles and we return to the van. Inside, eyes peek at me from the rearview mirror, and I start to feel nervous. Kitra holds my hand.

"Why did you move from Israel?" she calmly asks the driver, trying hard to make conversation.

"My wife did not like it," the driver responds, curtly. He flips on the stereo, sick of questions, and the lively prayer songs awaken all inside. Kitra's smile matches theirs.

"It's Rebbe Nachman," she informs me. "He advocates talking to God as you would with your best friend."

The holy words are spliced with electronic dance music. The truck shakes with spirit now as the men, and Kitra, holler ecstatically in Hebrew. I find the unabashed spirituality extremely comforting. I was raised to think spiritual expression was, at best, laughable, erroneous, embarrassingly naïve. I sway along with the foreign words, feeling calm.

Suddenly, the playlist jumps to nineties pop music: Pink, Jennifer Lopez, the Backstreet Boys, and 50 Cent, and to my delight the songs are greeted with almost as much reverence as the religious melodies.

"I'm comin' up so you better get this party started!" the driver shouts, the walls of the stretch van bulging with excitement.

After ten hours of travel we are nearing the Gathering, and everyone can feel it.

As we approach this year's site, I spot the now-familiar lineup of cars, the Blue Bird school buses and bumper stickers: *JESUS FREAK, STEAL YO FACE, MOTHER GAIA ON BOARD*. We are on the other side of the country, in an entirely different state from last time, but the setup looks surprisingly similar.

"Lovin' you!" a half-naked man on the road yells at our car.

The driver parks the stretch van on the roadside and we prepare for the trek down to Main Circle. A few cars drive by with people asking us for cigarettes, but nobody has any to offer. Despite the visual similarities here, I feel very different than I did before. We're not traveling with Jesse and Sticky but with a pack of ominous Rainbow newbies. We expertly ditch the men en route to Main Meadow, thanking them for the ride and wishing them well. We never did have to pay for gas and are grateful for their help.

On the hike down, we run into a wide assortment of Rainbows: a wild-eyed man hands out flyers on veganism; a young girl holds a sign reading *Bliss Ninja Needs a Hand*. A group of goth teens huff solvents from torn Walmart bags. We cross elaborate hand-built bridges, stray rock sculptures, flailing hippie children clutching crystals, clothes adorned in Deadhead patches. There's an acrid smell of sewage wafting over the settlement.

Once we reach Main Circle, we check the hand-drawn map and try to orient ourselves. Although some camps from last year have returned, we're surprised to find there is no Dirty Kids Camp this year, no Turtle Soup. We aren't sure yet which new camp has swallowed these crowds, so we wait and watch. We pitch our tent apart from everyone, in the forest behind a Jewish camp called Shtetl Kettle. Kitra wants to plan our attack, but I feel detached and tired. Although I'm eager to keep following the story, I begin to remember that traveling isn't easy. In fact, it's exhausting and emotionally challenging. A giant black man dressed as a leprechaun standing on the path spots me sulking and asks if I need a hug.

"Yeah," I say. "I do."

He holds me tight, stable, unflinching. "I love you, sister," he says, and I smile. "Welcome home."

THE FOLLOWING MORNING, we eat our peanut butter and plan. We want to keep taking portraits, find new kids, and make traveling connections. As we walk down the dirt path to Main Meadow, we spot Useless for the first time since last summer and are ecstatic to see a familiar face. He is hustling for used coffee grounds to make his famous "mud" drink. As we approach, we hear him talking to someone about the perception of Gatherings in Babylon.

"We're taught it is safer in Babylon than in the woods," he says to a disheveled, nodding woman sitting beside him. "There ain't nothing wrong with the woods!"

"Hey!" I interrupt, excitedly. "Do you remember us? We took photos of your wedding last year."

Useless's face changes, lighting up.

"Welcome home, sisters! Right on!"

We ask him where Misty Dawn is, his wife from the pagan handfasting ceremony. He looks sullen. He says she has left him. We offer our condolences and agree it was a beautiful wedding.

"Four weeks after we wed, she went home. She couldn't handle the bus, traveling all the time."

I can relate. Useless tells us that in between Gatherings, he drives a bus he calls Montana Mud from city to city. This bus acts as a nomadic heroin treatment center for poor folks looking to get clean. I spy his large brown bus, dusty and dark, and think how beautiful this idea is.

He begins calling out for coffee grounds again, like a manic auctioneer. "Bring us your coffee grounds and we will make you mud! This ain't coffee, it's *mud*!"

Useless thanks us for the photos we brought him in our pack. With his permission, we set up a photo booth at the intersection of River Rats and Montana Mud Camp: these two camps seem to be the meeting place for tramps, train hoppers, and teenage runaways, comparable to the Dirty Kids Camp of last summer. Although faces are different, this subset of Rainbows remains similar: kids have face tattoos, torn clothes, and chained pit bulls.

Within a few minutes of settling in, a giggling intoxicated girl sits besides me, introducing herself as Crosswalk. She is gorgeous, with light-brown skin, bright-white teeth, and a half-shaved head. She's dressed like the Statue of Liberty in an American-flag bikini, white cloak, and crown. She's eager to talk to me after Kitra and I explain what we're doing. I take out my audio recorder and apologize for putting it kind of close to her face.

"That's okay," she says, chuckling. "I've seen many shrinks."

"Me too," I concede, comforted, and we laugh together like old friends.

I wonder what my psychiatrists would make of me now; which useless diagnoses would be added to my case file if I disclosed my newfound wanderlust. *Diagnonsense.*

Crosswalk talks to me in manic bursts, speaking into the microphone. "I'm eighteen. I just hit the road a month ago. I met this Rainbow scout who offered to fix up my dreadlocks in Washington Harbor. I just got out of work with the Census Bureau, so it was perfect timing. I busted out of a recovery house that night."

I've been told that Rainbow scouts are Family members that infiltrate inner-city areas, searching for possible future Rainbows, for those in need of a place to stay. Sometimes these searches are specifically geared to recruiting nonwhite Rainbows, including African Americans, other people of color, and ethnic minorities. Crosswalk happened to meet one of these scouts during her recovery and decided to travel with him instead of continuing her recovery. Sober Rainbow camps exist, such as Jesus Camp, and are run to support more vulnerable and recovering Family members. But Crosswalk is not camping with the sober camp. She continues talking without being prompted.

"When I first hit the road, it was a culture shock and I was crying a lot. At one point, I woke up in a fucking bathtub that wasn't mine, crying and licking up the bathwater, on Klonopin and alcohol. I figured out that's not a good mixture. On the road, you got to find the right mixture of drugs and sobriety. It's all about balance to stay safe and healthy. My journal is my best friend, and my puppy is my best friend, too, because I figured, fuck human beings and fuck being alone, too. So, my dog is my best friend. I named him Clay."

A thin naked man rolls a joint in his sticky lap beside us. Crosswalk's vibrant energy is intoxicating. She's new to the Rainbow scene but has adapted quickly. Her new road dog, Clay, a small puppy, ambles up to her, coughing and growling.

"I found my dog at a parking lot of a Walmart being sold by

some Mennonites, at seven weeks old. He was an expensive pup, you could tell because his tail was docked. I paid $250 for him, the last of my money pretty much."

When I ask her why she is dressed as the Statue of Liberty, she says she was supposed to get married earlier in the day but decided against it. She picked up her costume at Trade Circle but got sick of her new boyfriend real quick and decided against the marriage.

"There's a Nic at Night. Do you know what that is?"

Nic at Nights are folks who run around Rainbowland offering free tobacco to Family: they both take donations and dole out smokeables to those in need. Emphatic "Nic at Night!" calls can often be heard across the entire site. When I tell her I'm familiar with Nic at Nights, Crosswalk continues talking about her fiancé.

"I heard he called himself 'Nig at Night,' because he's black. I proposed to him as a joke, he fell in love, and we were going to get married. I said I was going to dress up like the Statue of Liberty because we were going to have a parade marriage. But I called off the wedding. I don't really like him that much at all..."

Scanning her patriotic costume, I ask Crosswalk how she feels about the state of the U.S. and she laughs.

"Jesus. I don't know. I like the colors red white and blue. I don't fucking know. I really don't like politics. My family is really political. I see what it's done to my sister. It's made her really stressed out and serious. I play by my own rules."

She immediately tears up when I ask more about her family.

"I think about my family a lot. I call my dad as much as I can. My parents are still together, so if I call my dad, Mom hears... I'm not allowed there. I got kicked out because I cause him so much emotional trauma because I don't play by the rules ever."

Someone from the Montana Mud kitchen passes out a tray of "zuzus," chocolate-covered treats, for everyone to share.

Desperate to escape from a Rainbow gone wrong, young travelers try their luck hitchhiking out of Rainbowland.

PENNSYLVANIA, JULY 2010

"I fucking love it here, dude. I'm so fucking grateful. This is home! There's so much fucking love, and especially this Rainbow, I hear, has a lot of love. Man, for the fucking nomad that you're so interested in, this place is heaven. This place is home because I don't have a home anymore." Crosswalk tears up again. "Fuck NA! That shit works if you work it, but this shit works if you love it!"

As someone who has struggled with mental illness and substance use, I know unconditional acceptance is often more healing than following strict rules or deferring to an outside authority.

THE NEXT MORNING, I wake at dawn, aching to urinate. I unzip the tent and scuttle out in the darkness, searching for a place to piss. I walk absentmindedly beside a dugout ditch near our tent, and I fall in. My feet slide over leaves and mud and human waste and I gag, disgusted. Sanitation is a key concern at all Gatherings, an aspect folks do not take lightly. You will often hear a chorus of "Cover your shit!" when you're passing through a kitchen, a safety precaution and reminder that is one of the only real rules in Rainbowland. This call refrains constantly at camps in order to get the message across—people shout it to everyone who passes, whether they are heading to relieve themselves or not. It's simple: if you don't cover your waste, flies will land, lay eggs, and spread illness. Everyone will get sick. Well-organized camps ensure the toilet areas are located downwind. These areas are often marked, depending on the camp and Gathering. Rainbow works because it makes you consider your everyday actions; it makes you confront your own excrement face on. It makes you realize that you are a consumer and a defecator, and forces you to take responsibility for this fact.

On the fourth day of Rainbow, Kitra and I hand out journals: small blank ships with pens attached and notes reading *Return to River Rats When Full.* Strangers pour out their life experiences on paper. One paper ship returns early. On the front page, written in a scrawl, it reads:

> *When I started out on the road last November I was traveling with a chunk of money that I happened to have from a car-wreck settlement. That is one kind of traveling, when you have a fat bank account to rely on. There was a certain relief when the money ran out in April. I had been preoccupied with the fear that I was spending it too quickly or imprudently. But we had seen people all along the way making it with nothing but their attitudes and inner resources. I am becoming one of those people. Enough is enough, or rather, enough is plenty. I am living out the dream I had since I was a little kid and I am bound to no one. The fears just fall away if you sit with them long enough.*

Most journals are lost in the sea of Rainbows, never returned.

GRANDPA WOODSTOCK, AN eighty-year-old man dressed in a frilly unbuttoned shirt, penis exposed, stands in the center of Main Meadow. Rainbows give him high fives and hugs, and he walks around smiling, senile, drooping, loved. His wife, Grandma Woodstock, stands beside him, with a long staff of facial hair. Everyone is gathered around them for the annual Prayer for Peace ceremony, which they are helping to lead. Grandpa Woodstock has just married three young couples, who are now necking joyously in the field. We all hold hands and form a circle to start the prayer. Although this Gathering is smaller than the one in New Mexico, the familiar om-ing begins and I close my eyes, hopeful. Remembering last year I feel peace blanket me.

"Om," I chant, openly this time. "Om!"

My nose is suddenly filled with the vile scent of rotten eggs. I open my eyes and see a colorful streak of smoke flit across the field, into the center of our circle. A stink bomb explodes.

"Fuck you, Rainbows!" a young voice screams. "You gay faggots! You child molesters!"

My eyes sting from the stink. Through blurry pupils, I see the Death Camp kids—a pack of six feral, unwashed, angry children, all under the age of eighteen. The oldest child holds a newborn baby strapped to her chest. Another, a boy around the age of ten, is cross-eyed, dressed in a skimpy evening gown. He continues his tirade, vehemently.

"Next time you have a meeting about us, maybe you should invite us to come!"

I learn there had been a counsel meeting to discuss how to deal with this unruly camp of children. I think back to Michael Niman's book, where he notes the Gathering is run on the principal of "zenanarchy," in which individual choice is emphasized, group consensus is practiced, and peacekeeping is paramount. Problems are dealt with in exhaustive group counsels, where everyone is invited to speak and participate, and voices are mediated by passing a "magic feather" around for hours, even days.

Folks unlink arms and there is an argument about how to proceed. A hippie riot erupts, putting the prayer on hold.

"He could have blasted someone's eye out!" shouts a man, advancing on the kids.

"What they need is love!" one woman shouts. "Let us help them!"

"You're all child molesters!" the boy in the dress shouts again. "Fucking child molesters!"

A group of peace-hungry hippies surround the Death Camp kids, forming an odd-looking circle around them, still holding hands.

"Om!" they shout, almost aggressively. "Om!"

The boy in the dress tries to kick and claw his way out of the trap but is restrained. Biting and kicking, the children finally break through the wall of sound. They toss another colorful stink bomb as they retreat into the forest. Shaken, the Main Meadow group tries to recover. Some attempt to resume their Prayer for Peace but give up quickly. After ten minutes, watermelon is distributed to a sullen crowd.

After the Prayer for Peace, I run into Moe, Sicka's girlfriend from the New Mexico Gathering. She's walking around the meadow, playing a mini accordion, singing like a swallow. I ask her if she's still dating Sicka and she laughs, saying she moved on long ago.

"She's a heroin junkie," she says.

I say nothing—I had no idea she was still using. I feel sad, though not surprised. Moe shrugs and walks off into the crowd, squeezing her accordion in and out.

Back at Montana Mud later that evening, the dirty kids laugh off the prank, inviting the Death Camp kids in for zuzus near the campfire. Useless seems somewhat apathetic about the whole situation. The darkness doesn't disturb him like it does many other Rainbows. I begin asking around about Death Camp and find a variety of explanations and stories:

"I hear they stabbed their babysitter."

"They live wild, in the woods, without parents."

"They're just a pack of disrespectful yokels. They ruin things every year."

TWO KIDS STAND at our portrait booth. One calls himself Spit, and his traveling companion goes by the name Lora Galora. Kitra reminds me that she had taken their portraits back in New Mexico, but now they are almost unrecognizable. Lora has transformed from a blonde, cherubic young girl to a full-blown traveler, with a mash of new tattoos and a shaved head. Spit's hair is longer and matted, and his face is covered in tattoos. It's astounding to see such a stark transformation in only a year. I feel somewhat awkward, or perhaps jealous, as I'm fairly confident I look exactly the same as I did last year, and I wonder if this is a good or bad thing.

"Actually, I already saw these on the Internet," Lora confesses when we give her a copy of her portrait. Kitra's photos from New Mexico have garnered worldwide attention, winning awards from the World Press Photo Foundation. "It's just funny, to see me with hair. It's been a while. From here I had dreadlocks, then a dread mullet," she says, pointing to the portrait. "Got lice and so I cut the rest of my mullet off."

"What's changed since we last met?" I ask her.

"Well, I started riding trains, so that's probably been the biggest change this year. And really just traveling, being able to sustain myself without feeling like I'm stressed out by traveling or feeling like I need to stop or anything."

Train hopping is a core, and controversial, method of travel for the American nomad. It often separates the wheat from the chaff, the weekend warriors from the hardcore full-time travelers. Riding trains is a dirty, dangerous mode of transportation that often ends in death or disfigurement—many travelers at Rainbow have missing limbs, which stand in testament.

As a woman on the road, Lora doesn't feel particularly unsafe, I discover.

"I've had, like, one wing-nut ride, and even then he was just a wing nut and nothing bad actually happened. He was just crazy. I've actually gotten so comfortable with traveling and everything that this summer, if the opportunity presented itself, I'd definitely travel by myself. I just feel like I know what to do, you know?" Lora laughs. "As a female, I always have a knife on me. I've never had to use it for anything other than spreading peanut, but it just helps me feel protected."

I don't carry a knife myself. Kitra and I had considered carrying pepper spray but never picked any up, worrying about our constant Canada–U.S. border hops. Neither of us wanted to waste money on something we would have to toss away before heading back to Canada. But the contrast between feeling safe and feeling unsafe is a theme that has occupied my thoughts since last summer. My anxiety ensures I always feel somewhat unsafe, regardless of the scenario. I've never felt particularly unsafe traveling with Kitra, or among Rainbows, despite their rough edges. I wonder how other travelers cultivate stable feelings of safety, if they feel safer moving or staying still.

When I ask Spit how long he's been on the road, he tells me a year straight. He says he's thinking of heading south to ride motorcycles with a friend.

"I just want to go everywhere. It's boring being in the same city and doing the same thing every day." For money, Spit relies on the generosity of others. "People just give me shit. I've gotten three one-hundred-dollar kickdowns 'cause of my dog. She doesn't look hungry or nothing, they just see her and like her and give me money. I was at this show the other day and this guy—I didn't have a ticket, I was just going to hang outside—he just saw me and came up to me and gave me a ticket. He, like, knew what I was about and knew what I was doing."

"What are you about?" I ask him.

"Traveling. I hitchhike and ride freight. And, uh, seeing everything—that's what I'm about. Going everywhere."

Spit has some strong opinions on the sedentary life of modern Americans. "If you have to [stay still] because you have a kid or something, or you're in school, understandable. But if not, what the fuck are you doing with your life? Why not *do* something and *see* something, if you do not have anything tying you down? I was a trainer at Panera Bread. Same thing every day: just drink, work, drink, work. It sucked. It's boring. They worked the fuck out of me for no pay. And then some traveling kids came in and I fuckin' left. Like, fuck that!"

I can relate to Spit's annoyance with mainstream, sedentary life. Since last summer, I've had a harder time seeing myself

Police and park rangers are treated as participants by some Rainbow Family members, while others mark their appearance with a cautionary call of "Seven-up!"

PENNSYLVANIA, JULY 2010

staying in one city, one apartment. I've lusted for travel often since returning to Vancouver. Yet there's something holding me back from traveling full time. I mostly worry about my own stability on the road—if I'll be able to sustain travel, or if I'll end up arrested or in a loony bin, locked away. I ask Spit if he's gotten a lot of shit for traveling, if he's ever gotten abuse from the police.

"Yeah. Oh, yeah. Oh, police, every fucking day! Once I got my name writ four times in this same on-ramp trying to hitchhike in this illegal place. In Chicago, there's these punk rock kids that light your sleeping bag on fire, stab you, and fucking kill you if you are a squatter kid 'cause they are so punk rock. They, like, rip your dreads out of your head, steal your dog—like, fucking kill you... Yes, you're dirty, you're homeless? You don't have rights. It's simple: you get fucked."

This statement fills me with rage, having experienced harassment from cops firsthand all of my life. It also makes me fearful of the wild nomads we have yet to meet. The drums and chanting in the field beside us amplifies. I ask Spit if he's going to be in Washington for the next Rainbow and he scoffs.

"Nah, I don't really do Gatherings anymore. I just do Ocala nationals. Ocala is the shit. Go to Ocala, Florida. Get there around the end of January, beginning of February. Valentine's Day is the main big day. It's the shit. It's awesome. Best Gathering I have ever been to. I like getting together with friends and stuff, and that's what Ocala is, just road dogs, like, street kids, and traveling kids and real people and shit. It's tight."

"Road dogs" is another name for travelers, and a term to signify your main traveling partner. Spit and Lora Galora are road dogs, and Kitra and I are road dogs. I wonder when we will attend Ocala—this year or next. I thank him and Lora for the interviews.

LATER THAT DAY, I interview a man near a campfire who goes by the name One Leg Mike, because, I assume, he only has one leg. I have heard some Rainbow Gatherings have been canceled because of the environmental damage they have done to fragile ecosystems and I want to hear about this firsthand from someone who's set up and torn down. Mike is often part of Seed Camp and teardown, and we found him while walking the hand-forged trails that crisscross Rainbowland. Mike also helps run a camp called Shark Bait, an Alabaman-themed kitchen that has been around for about five years. He has traveled on a number of kitchen buses, including one called the Gus Bus, and is the one to talk to about the topic of bus life and nomadic kitchens. He speaks openly when I ask for an interview, with a gaggle of travelers congregated around him on the forest floor.

"We travel around and scavenge food from places, and then go and feed it to people for free," he explains. "It's a very unorganized system: there's no leader-people—there's a core group, but new people are coming in all the time, bringing in fresh energy. It keeps people from burning out."

I'm curious about how the kitchens and sanitation systems function from a practical standpoint, and without me even asking, Mike continues talking.

"Feeding at Rainbow is about service and making sure it gets done. A lot of people have different themes to their kitchen. We do a lot of deep-fried foods and our vibe is a little raucous—we're very loud, almost to the point of being obnoxious. We're very harsh on people and we come off very harsh about things like pooping, washing your hands, and all these things—sanitation issues. But really it's about keeping our family safe. So if we come off harsh, if we come off rude, or if we come off like aggro train kids, it's only because that kind of stuff people listen to. In an environment of love, when you get a harsh judgment-style thing pointed at you, you have to examine it, you have to examine where it comes from. And people don't listen to, like, 'Hey brother, can you blah blah blah for me?'"

Hearing this statement, two camp members a couple feet away start screaming, "Cover your shit!"

"Cover your shit!"

"COVER YOUR SHIT!"

Mike agrees with them. "Right! Bury your shit! Bury your dog's shit! Bury the bullshit!"

"Cover the horse's shit!" someone screeches from the woods. Even more members chime in, all around me. The noise is overwhelming and peppered with coughs and laughs and communal agreement.

"I'm not a person that would normally cuss. When I come into Rainbow, I scream, I yell at people, I let them know what has to happen. Being vocal about these things is what allows everyone to learn. A lot of people come out to Rainbow, and it's their first Gathering, and they don't really know how to exist out here. So they might not have a sleeping bag or they might not know how to wash their hands properly after they use the bathroom, and that can be a danger to everyone out here. When you have Gatherings like nationals, they can be huge. [At some nationals] there's been one, two, three, four, five shitters dug up a hill, and [at one Gathering] two of them were giant—100 percent huge trench shitters, and this Gathering specifically we had a lot of issues with the underground water. You can't dig down too far because you don't want to go beyond the clay level and get poop into the ground water. Right now, where we're sitting is an underground river. So sanitation for the Family and sanitation for the forest [is important]—keeping the forest clean, keeping the water clean, so that we don't leave a negative impact on the environment."

He tells me about all the efforts Rainbows make to ensure they leave no trace: break up all the trails, plant fresh seeds, and pick up "microtrash," or pocket trash. It is people like Mike who set up during Seed Camp and stick around during cleanup. It is these people who create and maintain Rainbow.

A man sitting beside Mike pipes up. "This is our lives: we live in the woods, we do this all the time. But when something goes down in Babylon where people need some help, we're already equipped to do it."

To my surprise, he tells me that Rainbow Family members are often involved in disaster relief. And many buses function to feed people in inner-city parks and slums using dumpstered and donated supplies.

One Leg Mike continues. "So much food is wasted in America. The culture of excess that is developed based on capitalism creates an abundance of waste. And that abundance really translates into a lot of food."

He describes how some companies will even donate food to them, knowing they do good work—such as when a tofu company donated a ton of tofu ten months after Katrina to bring to New Orleans' Ninth Ward, before, according to Mike, the Federal Emergency Management Agency (FEMA) had even set up a proper response, and while the city was still having problems with general sanitation. He also mentions how his bus went down to the Gulf of Mexico to help out with the oil spill disaster relief there, feeding volunteers and helping with cleanup.

"You think Rainbow is anarchistic and everyone can do their own thing, and that's true. But there's structure. There's structure, but it's not a fascist structure, because you don't have some sort of authoritarian order that's controlling it. Everyone knows what has to be done, and everyone is their own educator, and everyone is vocal about what they need and what has to happen for the Family, and that's what it takes. It takes clear communication and action. With those two things, you can get a lot of shit done."

I feel astounded and inspired, hopeful, as I see anarchist ideals being practiced so eloquently—and in reality.

IT'S BEEN A week, and the Gathering is winding down. Kitra and I need to find a ride back into Babylon. We head to Bus Village, where all the school buses and RVs are parked. On the way, we stop by a Christian trailer giving out potato chips and grape drinks. We have worked nonstop all week, photographing and interviewing seemingly all day and night. Kitra does not seem the least bit tired, but I'm exhausted, sunstruck, and irritable. We hear the Grateful Dead wafting through the air, and we search for buses that will give us a ride out. Kitra is still intent on finding another group of kids, to stretch out our scope, to keep working. She talks with kids sprawled out underneath a school bus while I sit by the side of the road alone, sulking, ready to go home, to get comfort, to take a bath.

Eventually, after failing to find another contact, Kitra surrenders, and we lug our gear up the steep hill. We hang out at A-camp looking for a ride out. We've been warned to stay away from A-camp. It's the site of almost all of the violence in Rainbowland, including numerous stabbings over the years. A-camp is the only place in Rainbowland where alcohol is permitted. Although weed is smoked freely almost anywhere in Rainbowland, drinking and hard drugs are taboo. According to the Perkel Rainbow Gathering Mini Manual, an unofficial online Rainbow guide, "All forms of intoxication can be harmful to the spirit of our gathering." Alcohol is seen as a by-product of Babylon that incites rage and hatred. "Personalities can change on alcohol (and hard drugs). Sometimes people can't control themselves as well. Therefore you are respectfully asked to leave the alcohol in A-camp when you hike into the main gathering space." Other items suggested to be left at A-camp are aggressive dogs, bad attitudes, hard drugs, radios, and guns, which are never really welcomed at the Gathering. Weed, however, is seen more as a spiritual aid or medicine versus an intoxicant. Kitra and I wonder, however, if most of the A-camp violence is overblown, sensationalist fuel for the local news media stuck on demonizing Rainbow intruders. Multiple stabbings, murders, and rapes, however, have been reported in the last few years, the details of which I will learn more about as I get to know more travelers.

A-camp is a scatter of trailers and barrel fires. A woman with dilated pupils looks past us into nothingness. Paranoid gazes peek from busted trailers and trucks, smoke billowing through cracks and windows. Suspicious chemical smells leak from windows. Without any obvious leads for a ride, we keep walking. At the top of the hill, back on the main road, we try to find a ride. An RV stops and lets us in within minutes. For hours, Kitra talks to the man about Judaism and I sit in the back, head jangling back and forth, trying to regroup, to get myself together. I feel exhausted, angry, and pathetic, and I don't know why. I think about the Death Camp kids, shouting, angry, and wild. I think about all the interviews I recorded. My anxiety is off the charts. I feel sick to my stomach. For the first time during these travels, I feel somewhat unsafe, or at least unstable—not because of the people I am surrounded with but because of the state of my own mind. The RV drops us off at a train station and we spend the night sleeping on a bench in the open air. I lie awake and think about Useless. I wonder how many couples the road has pulled apart. It's damp and I drift to sleep wondering why I can't cope like Kitra.

CHAPTER 5

‖‖‖‖‖‖‖‖‖‖‖

Sand Fleas

(JULY 2010)

W E'RE BACK AT Kitra's sister's sublet on the Upper East Side and there are piles of clothing everywhere. I throw everything I own into the washing machine and spend an hour in the shower. Kitra doesn't wash her hair. Sal messages us, saying he's also in New York, playing a show tonight in Brooklyn at a place called Otto's Shrunken Head. He's no longer with the 12 Shades of Schwilly Silly and is now in a band called Up Up We Go! This is good timing. Kitra and I want to move forward with our project, to catch up with the kids we met in New Mexico a year prior. We still have our gear from last week's Gathering in Pennsylvania and want to take more portraits and record more interviews. We are eager to learn how nomads live within the limits of Babylon. I feel nervous about seeing Sal again. Sicka messaged me recently on MySpace to tell me she had a "bone to pick." I called her up, long distance, in Seattle, where she was living.

"Wow, you actually called," she said upon picking up the phone, shocked.

"Of course I did. What's going on?"

Sicka informed me that all the kids are totally pissed about the article for *COLORS*.

"You made the whole Gathering look like it was just dirty kids," she explained, "which it isn't."

I was confused: Was she not camping at Dirty Kids Camp? Was there something wrong with showing the rougher, dirtier, less hippie-dippie side of Rainbowland?

"Those were the camps where we were hanging out at," I said, choking up. Hearing how upset I was, Sicka's tone changed drastically.

"Look, whatever," she said. "Don't worry about it. I can tell you really care about this whole thing. It's really not such a big deal."

After the phone call, I was devastated: Were any of the others angry? Would they want to continue traveling with us? Then came the harder questions: Who was I to tell this story? Did I have any right? Where did my voice fit in, anyway?

It's no surprise that word of the photos had spread quickly among the dirty kids. Social media is intertwined with the life of the young nomad; many travelers keep in touch digitally in some way or another, whether through Facebook or email, or, in the past, MySpace, ICQ, or MSN. Many kids use friends' computers, and many have smartphones themselves. The Internet has added another novel level of transparency and immediacy to our documentation process—kids can see their photos as soon as they're uploaded, read teaser articles as soon as they're published, find out which friends have been arrested through online news reports (something I experienced when I found mug shots of Sal, Thaddeus, and Frankie published online after they were arrested for sleeping on a roof).

Three hours later, we're sitting at the bar at Otto's Shrunken Head, the type of place where you buy twenty-dollar drinks with pom-poms and sparklers and weird plastic shit hanging off the rim. Beside us at the bar, a plump thirtysomething couple orders a Shrunken Head special: a vat of windshield cleaner–blue slush served in a glass as big and round as a fishbowl, with sparklers vomiting up flames along the rim. Plastic ornaments wink from across the bar, tacky and hyper. We order sodas and wait for Sal. Kitra doesn't drink, so I try to refrain when I'm with her.

I notice a figure heading up to the stage, setting up instruments. His hair is long, tied up in a greasy bun at the top of his head. Tattered purple vest with a third-eye decal on the back, jagged raccoon tail peeking out atop a pair of short shorts, the same *Voodoo Hand* tattoos, dark skin, and large chestnut eyes. It's the first time we've seen Sal since publishing our article and I can feel my stomach turn; I'm uneasy after speaking with Sicka. When Sal spots us, he runs over and embraces us warmly, instantly, like family.

"It was crazy," he says. "Seeing my face like that in a magazine! I even showed my mom!" He giggles, then his face turns sad. "Those are the only photos I have of Dapper Dan. He's dead."

Apparently, after Sal left his dog with some friends during a recent trip, Dapper Dan was hit by a car. He tells us his friends stuffed the dog's carcass. I can't tell if this displeases or comforts him.

Eli sits in the corner in a knee-length corduroy dress, seeming gloomy but still friendly. He's sitting with a woman around our age, twenty or so. She has a buzz cut, red-striped shirt, and broken arm in a cast and sling. She sucks on a breath-activated keytar. I note the slew of brown birthmarks covering her skin, faint splotches that make her body look like a beautiful human globe. Before we have a chance to speak, she heads to the stage. The set starts and the three of them begin shrieking.

"The children are dancing, but we don't know why!"

The group sings and blows, undulating, alive, on fire. Their act is infectious. Josh is out of the picture, it seems, and the woman with the buzz cut is now tearing up the stage.

"That asshole shot heroin in my mom's bathroom," Sal later explains of Josh, revolted. "Left the syringe in there and everything." Sal hates heroin, as his father was an addict. Booze, weed, Molly, LSD—those are different stories.

Outside the bar after the show, a crowd of crusty punks have assembled. They're chugging booze from cranberry juice containers and sharing hand-rolled cigarettes. They don't have money for cover to get into the bar and are sitting on the sidewalk, spanging for beer. We sit down with Skunk, a kid with blue vine tattoos covering the right side of his face. He's traveling with Janessa and Vulture, a punk couple with a pit bull. Janessa has a Tank Girl haircut, and Vulture sports a chin strap tattoo. They're around twenty years old.

"Oogles are deeply annoying," Janessa spits, staring at us as soon as we sit down beside them.

"Oogle," I learn, is a derogative term for a hanger-on hipster who tries to act tough like a traveler but has money or a home and a whole other life. In other instances, it is simply a term for a shitty traveling punk who makes a mess and blows up a spot for others. A trustafarian could be seen as an oogle, for example, as could a journalist following a story. I shift self-consciously in my ripped jeans. I know she thinks I'm an oogle—a well-meaning one, but one nonetheless—and it's clear she's calling me out, testing me. We're not rich, but we have the funds we raised online; we have options. I have a family back home, with money, a cottage, a hot tub.

Her bubbly, chatty boyfriend, Vulture, contradicts Janessa's attitude. He smiles and welcomes us openly.

"Spare a high five?" he shouts at a passerby.

A middle-aged couple approaches, visibly tipsy, from down the street.

"Tell us about your date!" Vulture insists as they pass, much more interested in the ins and outs of their relationship than bumming a dime.

"Oh, it was fantastic," replies the woman, a round lady in a skintight striped minidress. She tells us her name is Marge. "Candlelight, wine, beautiful!"

"What are you guys doing here, then?" her boyfriend asks, friendly but assertive, in a thick New Yorker accent. He's wearing an American-flag T-shirt. "What, are you just *hangin' out*?"

Vulture explains how they are traveling through the U.S., that this is one of their first nights in New York City. Soon enough, Marge decides this is fantastic and wants to take the whole lot of us for a drink down the street.

"Just one beer!" she shouts, and leads us happily to Blarney Cove, where she orders us a couple pitchers. The kids raise their cups ecstatically. At the bar, I sit next to Marge, who is encased in her sausage dress, unsteady on her barstool. She turns to me.

"Hey," she says, "can I tell you a secret?"

I say yes. I'm used to people asking me this question. I'm getting used to functioning as a human confessional. Strangers have always talked to me, but the more interviews I conduct, the more people I find telling me their secrets.

"Deep down, I want to do what you guys are doing," Marge says. "Traveling, sleeping under the stars, adventure," she says. "I'm from South America. I miss the air, the nature, the movement. I'm sick of living in the city, this cage. I'm so sick of living this way."

Her brown eyes are earnest, desperate, hungry, busking. I nod. She doesn't know I'm an outsider, just like her. Her need for more movement is honest. After her confession, Marge and her man leave the bar, drunk and ready for bed, and the kids remain at the bar without them. The staff is pissed.

"They dumped out my beer when I went to the can," Vulture whines. "I even asked the bartender to keep an eye on it! I don't think they're feeling us anymore."

Outside, Sal and Eli have set up a busking station and are bursting with song, staring into each other's eyes, riffing excitedly.

Monique greets the early-morning sun after sleeping on Brighton Beach.

NEW YORK, AUGUST 2010

I'm introduced to Maray Fuego—the female singer and keytar player—and learn she is a traveler from Michigan. She is also the composer of many of the songs I've already heard at Rainbows past (including "I Fucking Hate Money," sung by Elanor in New Mexico). She and Sal go way back, having traveled together through the South and beyond. A sloppy drunk woman comes outside where the kids are busking to tell us we are disturbing the business, that we can't play music there, that we have to go somewhere else.

"Don't get me wrong, you guys are great, you just can't play here."

The kids return home to vans, rooftops, and dingy New York bachelors, piled atop one another to sleep. Kitra and I return to the Upper East Side, enlivened and eager to keep documenting.

New York City might be the furthest you can get from Rainbowland. The last time I'd been here was a few years back, when Kitra and I asked her father to drive us from Montreal so that we could interview carnival workers at Coney Island. It was the first time Kitra and I had worked together, just a feature for our university newspaper, but our trip solidified our working relationship.

My obsession with nomads started with carnies. I'd idealized carnival workers since I was a child, after watching workers tend the rides at the annual Massey Fair I attended every summer in Northern Ontario. I saw carnies as mythical creatures: nomadic, mysterious, excitingly sexy, commendably counterculture. Carnies were everything I was not. They could leave whenever they wanted, look how they wanted; they were free. As I got older, my passion for carnival folk only intensified. When asked whether I was considering studying law or medicine by my parents' straitlaced friends, I often responded that my actual interest was "riding the rails with my carnival brothers and sisters," a response I intended to be both humorous and dismissive. I started to study the history of the carnival tradition and bask in the splendor of such a gritty and misunderstood underworld. Carnies were some of the original American nomads. For me, Coney Island's Astroland was the pinnacle of this subculture, an amusement park with an unparalleled history of carnival magic. So back at McGill, when Kitra and I first took to researching and pursuing stories on our own, we found out that a large part of Coney Island was being bought out by Thor Equities and we traveled to NYC to interview the workers. This was a formative experience. Coney carnies are a dying breed, and I'm lucky to have talked to many. Although the park remains, the grit and grime of Coney Island was largely cleaned up, and many carnies were sent packing.

"MEMORY IS A funny thing," Maray Fuego tells me on the L train to Brighton Beach, a seaside neighborhood on the Coney Island peninsula, later that week. "I don't have one anymore."

I point out the cast on her arm.

"I got it playing cello behind my head," she says to me. "No, wait, I got it wrestling an alligator."

I picture Maray, this noble road warrior, with closed fists, wringing the neck of a gasping gator. The truth, I eventually find out, is she fell off a porch while blackout drunk. This is why she's playing a blow keytar and not her usual accordion. It's not necessarily a common occurrence for Maray, but it happened, and now there's a cast and a hole in her head where the memory should be.

We spend the day watching Up Up We Go! busking illegally in Williamsburg, a gaggle of travelers clustered together playing kazoos and banjos. Tom Waits, Memphis Minnie, original songs, and old Disney tunes. The hipster passersby seem impressed, throwing dollars into Sal's open case, while we keep our eyes out for cops. Skunk, the kid with the blue vines down his face, puffs on a small portable flute. Maray does another rendition of her song "I Fucking Hate Money":

"You count your pennies, and I'll throw my pennies to the trash," she begins in a warbly voice. "You just want to save them and I just want to see them go flat."

As the chorus comes, everyone joins in: "I fucking hate money, I fucking hate money, I fucking hate money so much! It makes people greedy it makes people stingy it makes people keep all their stuff to themselves!"

After nightfall, Sal declares that it is his twenty-third birthday and he wants to go to Brighton Beach, despite the fact that it's midnight and nobody has bus fare. We've picked up another friend, Monique, a Betty Boop look-alike with pin-thin eyebrows. She talks about her strip act back in New Orleans, how she would take off her knee socks on the sidewalk for hours, a provocative performance piece she did for spare change.

We hop over the barriers in the Williamsburg subway station, triggering the alarm, which howls like a broken rooster. We all run through and onto the train together: Williamsburg, E8, Brooklyn.

A black man dressed in white with a keyboard sets up in our subway car. "Sal! What's up, brother?" he exclaims when we jump in the car.

"Hey, man!"

Sal knows him, most likely through busking, and excitedly they start playing a tune. Their ability to freestyle is impressive, and they feed off each other effortlessly. About ten stops into our ride, Maray and Eli decide they need to get off the train and see if one of their friends, Hannah, is around, stopping the music cold in its tracks. Hannah lives in a communal house with plenty of places to sleep, and such connections are valuable when you don't have access to a shower or bed.

"You're going to abandon me on my *birthday*?" Sal shrieks, shocked.

"Don't worry! We'll meet you at the beach," Eli assures him.

It's clear Eli is the one Sal is mad at, not Maray, and mad he most certainly is.

"Fine, go! I don't give a fuck," Sal shouts. And they do, out the electric doors without looking back.

The mood has clearly dropped. "I don't even feel like singing anymore," Sal says.

In silence, we ride out to the beach. We arrive at around one in the morning. The area is abandoned and sketchy. Spilled fruit covers the sidewalk. Shadowy people hide in corners. The kids want more booze, so we hit up a twenty-four-hour convenience store for forties.

"I'm worried about my camera," Kitra whispers to me, keeping it hidden in her bag. "This isn't a good part of town."

Seeing Kitra uneasy instantly puts me on edge, because it's the first time I've seen it. A middle-aged man comes up to us outside the corner store and introduces himself as Mike. He's red in the face and rambling.

"This is my neighborhood," he shouts. "Let me show you around."

The kids are friendly. Mike follows us to the beach. I feel anxious.

"Watch out for rigs," Vulture warns, and we scan the beach in the dark for needles before cuddling up together in the sand.

Monique whips off her shirt to expose a lacy see-through bra.

"Come on, Sally, let's go swimming!" she shouts.

"I'm not in the mood," Sal responds, still sour from Eli's earlier abandonment. "My mom doesn't like Eli. She says he toys with my heart," he laments into his forty.

We carve out body shapes in the sand, sinking into the warmth of the ground as the summer heat cools and the sea air turns colder. I watch the waves, the kids sipping on their forties, laughing, and smoking. Within a few minutes, two bodies approach us: Eli and Maray. Excited cheers come from the kids, but Sal remains angry.

"Where's Hannah?" he asks.

"We couldn't find her. Oh, come on, Sal, don't be mad," Eli says, a sexy smile curling up his face. "Don't be mad at me." He jumps onto Sal's lap and is instantly forgiven.

"You were the only one I was mad at," Sal confesses, pacified with Eli in his lap.

The energy lifts once again, and Sal rips off his clothes.

I start to feel small, sharp pricks on my skin. I scan the scene. Shady figures are all around us: on the horizon, in the water, beside us in the sand. We see a naked figure in the distance, wading in the dark water. Everyone dares Sal and Monique to approach him, and they do, drunkenly. We watch as they interact in the distance. My stomach curls into a ball. Fifteen minutes later, Sal and Monique return, shocked.

"He touched my penis!" Sal screams. "He touched my penis!"

"Oh, Christ, man. That is not cool. That is not okay," Mike, our self-appointed tour guide, says. "That is not okay."

Maray is working hard to cool him down, chatting pleasantly, changing the subject. He's drunk, uneasy and angry. Mike leaves for ten minutes. In his absence, people start talking about how freaky he's getting.

"Stop picking on him," Janessa says. "He didn't do anything wrong."

Mike returns with a container of raspberries he found in the trash and a metal pipe in his hand.

"I brought you a snack," he says, clutching the pipe.

I hold my breath.

Janessa approaches him, calmly, places a hand firmly on the pipe, looks directly into his eyes, and simply says, "No."

He lets go of the pipe.

I'm astounded by the kids' ability to negotiate violence and conflict, how their safety is a direct result of their ability to be confident and clearheaded in compromising situations, even while heavily intoxicated. I'm astounded at the group's ability to accept anyone that wants in, needs in, and needs a family or a home or a good chat.

As the sun goes down, I feel colder. Janessa borrows a plaid sweater from Skunk, but I'm too shy to ask for cover. We eat the garbage raspberries. The excitement has eased and kids are nodding off, catching a gloss of sleep before sunrise. I inch toward Kitra, who looks snug in her cheap black sweater. She is already asleep, breathing peacefully. I notice small red welts down the length of my legs and arms. I wonder if they are from rigs or bugs. The pinpricks, alien stings, heighten. *You are safe,* I tell myself. *You are okay.* This has become my interior mantra for whenever I feel uncomfortable, which is most of the time. *You are safe. You are okay,* I repeat until sunrise.

In the early light, regular people begin to filter onto the beach: joggers, swimmers, aged men with metal detectors. Some give us dirty looks, but most try to pretend we aren't there. In the morning sun, I inspect my limbs, which are dented red in many spots.

"Sand fleas?" Kitra asks.

In the U.S., they call these bloodsucking bugs by many different names: sand gnat, sand flea, no-see-um, granny nipper, chitra, punkie, or punky. They are seen as pests, parasites, a burning blight on a summer vacation. As the sun bumps above the horizon, none of the kids notice the bites, or if they do, none complain. They wake up from their light rests, finish up their piss-warm forties, and dart excitedly around the beach.

I interview Skunk, who tells me his real name is Jeremy. He starts by saying how much he hates the beach we're on—"It's the most hideous beach"—and I laugh, scanning the messy sand.

Skunk has been on the road for a long time. "I've been traveling for about, I'd say, fourteen years, on and off. I've gotten jobs, gotten my own place. But most of my life since, like, mid-teens has been spent either squatting in my hometown or on the road, traveling."

In that time, he's seen a lot of stuff on the road, both good and bad. "You know, people care about each other," he says. "People help each other out—people always help me out. I'd have to say the best things I've seen was just parts of the earth that aren't completely fucked up yet by people, that are like, you know, still semi-beautiful—shit grows, the water is still somewhat clean."

He continues, "And some of the worst things I've seen: what people do to the earth! They trash it, they litter it, they pollute it, they shit on it, they fuck it up. They're really good at fucking destroying things. That's kind of why I've developed the opinion that people are parasites. They're a bad thing, altogether. I mean, I've seen small examples of how people can live on the earth and live naturally and, you know, be self-sustainable, but the people of the earth as a mass majority are more pleased by materialism than, like, the simple life. They want things that they don't need, and those things that they don't need are produced, and the means that they're produced by destroy the earth, like, contribute to making life and sustainability on the earth more scarce as time goes by." Suddenly embarrassed, he chokes on his words.

I ask him if he considers himself a nomad, or if not, what he would call himself.

"I think at this point I'm just existing. I mean, I prefer to travel because over the years I've developed a network of people that I like to be around, people that I trust. My favorite time of the year is spring, because, like, the highlight of my life is going around and contributing to people's gardening, trying to encourage people to do more gardening and farming and shit like that, so that they're not so reliant on the capitalist system—which, you know, through feeding the masses they're destroying the earth. I try to play that small role with my existence and try to discourage people from being part of that. I'm doing the best I can. Most of the time, it feels good to do something that you know is right.

Then it feels really shitty when you look at something on a bigger scale and feel like, wow, you're really losing the battle, though. Things like the Gulf disaster just make me feel like I'm part of a doomed generation, maybe even part of some of the last human beings on earth—or, even worse, some of the last living things on earth."

I think about the Gus Bus, the Rainbow camp that traveled to the Gulf of Mexico to help clean up the mess after the oil spill without a second thought. Even though they had nothing, they dedicated their time to making dumpstered food for volunteers.

Skunk tells me he's been having a recurring dream that he wakes up one day with the woman he loves more than anything in the world (though he doesn't know who she is yet) and they are the last human beings on earth: "Sort of like Adam and Eve in the Bible, or whatever—you know, that shit." He is in charge of repopulating the earth. He tells me he looks around and the best thing he can think to do is kill both her and himself, to "end the human race and let the earth heal itself." He seems solemn, surprised by his own violence. "Any more questions?"

The kids on the beach are warming up, waking up, running around. Skunk looks sullen. "This beach really pisses me off," he says. "It was a lot better when it was too dark to see it all."

"Wow! Look at him!" Monique shouts, motioning to a young man doing laps in the surf.

She swims out to meet him in her see-through bra and panties, nipples exposed like brown figs. Monique brings the muscular man back to the group and he starts teaching Vulture some yoga poses, speaking in a deep Russian accent. Vulture, seemingly more drunk now that the sun is up, practices doing back flips off a stray log. The kids are writhing with laugher and he steps his act up, doing mock yoga moves, shoving handful after handful of beach sand in his mouth and swallowing.

"You are an idiot," Janessa says, angrily. "You are an idiot!"

Maray Fuego, Sal, and Eli from Up Up We Go! busk for rapt onlookers at First Avenue Station.

NEW YORK, AUGUST 2010

She has to spend the rest of the day with him, after all, and however many weeks to come. Vulture, now completely coated in sand, digs a hole around his crotch and lies down to pee.

"It works perfect!" he shrieks. "No one can see a thing!"

Eli and Sal play-wrestle on the beach, an adorably erotic sight, with Sal trying to push back against Eli's aggression, but not enough to stop his forwardness.

A few minutes later, Eli is pulling up his corduroy dress, asking someone to change the bandages on his bloody, blighted bare ass. "I've got a gnarly boil."

I eye his bubbly skin and feel revolted.

"I had one of those once," Skunk says. "Mine was from sitting on the streets too much."

I wonder what diseases and disfigurements I'm apt to catch on this trip. I try not to think about it.

Sand-covered and sleepy-eyed, we leave the beach, walking up the street to the subway, Monique still in her bra and panties.

"You're disgusting!" an elderly woman with a Russian accent shouts at us, her shirt buttoned up tightly. "You're absolutely disgusting."

The kids ignore her and keep walking. Vulture finds an abandoned baby stroller in the trash and asks the disgruntled Janessa to get in. He pushes her across the street in the ragtag pram, a guilty parent trying to make up for his negligence. At the subway station, we encounter a pack of cops. Instead of becoming nervous, the kids see this as part of the game.

"She's crippled!" they tell the cops. "She needs this thing to get around!"

The officers open the handicapped door, letting us onto the train, and continue chatting and sipping coffee, seemingly unfazed. Inside the train, the kids have a new energy, despite their lack of real sleep. Although I'm horrified by my new bites, I feel excited, too. Kitra looks exhausted and remains silent.

"If you come to my hood for breakfast, I'll pay," Monique shouts, and the kids agree.

They are hungry and so am I. We hop out the doors at our stop. Kitra wants to go home, and for the first time since we started, I don't. I return to the Upper East Side with her regardless.

THE NEXT MORNING, Kitra and I walk by Janessa and Vulture on a street corner in Brooklyn. Vulture is holding a stick tied to a can, spanging, fishing for money. Expecting a warm hello after last night's bonding, we flash them smiles. The pair look surly. They barely acknowledge us. I'm shocked and embarrassed, because we are nobody again.

We catch the subway to meet Sal, Maray, and Eli, and attend a house party at their friend Hannah's collective. Inside Hannah's there is mayhem: tons of rooms, helter-skelter, filthy, filled with paints and drugs and food and ratty furniture. The best part of the house is the huge piano in the main room, which Eli takes advantage of instantly, sitting down and carving out melodies from thin air.

A girl named Joy, whom none of the kids who live at the house know, walks up to the porch with a guitar case and traveling backpack, asking for Sal. Turns out she is a traveling musician, too, and has heard through the grapevine that Sal is back in New York. This is a common occurrence for Sal, and one of the main reasons he's getting kicked out of his current apartment—travelers constantly come in and out, needing a place to stay. And to say "no," especially when they have hosted you before, is blasphemy in the traveling scene. Joy whips out a banjo and begins singing in a Southern drawl. Her voice is steady and unafraid. I wonder where Joy developed such courage, to use the full power of her lungs. Where did these voices come from? I ask if I can record some of the music the kids are playing. I receive a sideways glance from Joy, but Eli comes to my rescue immediately.

"These guys are trustworthy," he says.

I am taken aback and my eyes well up.

"You are. You and Kitra are the most trustworthy people I know."

I have never felt more honored. It is an astounding feeling, especially after having felt like an absolute outsider for the majority of our trip so far—for the majority of my life, actually. The night deepens and the wine bottles and joints circulate. I work up the nerve to ask Maray if I can record an interview with her, and we head up to one of the tens of bedrooms in the house (at least I think it's a bedroom—there are newspapers and plates everywhere, so it might also serve as a kitchen). We seal the door shut to keep out the noise from downstairs. I ask her questions about being a woman on the road, and she opens up to me about her personal beliefs. She speaks in a jumpy way, questioning words that come out of her mouth, while maintaining a confident, almost gentlemanly, air, and begins to talk about her first traveling experience.

"I was seventeen and going to a lot of punk rock gatherings. And I went to one that was actually this pretty cool movement... it's like the way to get free education by having people who are educated just teach people. They had a bunch of workshops, so I took this one workshop that was on traveling... and was told by this girl who is awesome—she was really cool and she did a bunch of progressive stuff—I was like, 'Oh, how do you do what you do? Because I really am interested.' And she was like, 'You just do it.' And I was like, 'Oh.'"

She meows like a cat and we laugh. She starts talking about her experiences with anarchist collectives.

"And then a month later I went on my first hitchhiking trip... Me and one of my close friends hitched out to CrimethInc. Convergence in Winona, Minnesota... But it was really beautiful and it really made sense how easy it was to catch a ride. That was [when I] first thought, Oh you can get anywhere without money... if you start walking in a direction with an intention to get there. With any intention, if you just continue on that intention, it will come true. You know?"

She pauses for a minute when I ask her about the public perception of travelers.

"Some people might be afraid because they've been raised to think [life is] one way. You know what I mean? Raised to think they have a job as a secretary, or whatever they do... But I think that lots of people are breaking free. They're not necessarily going to be a watchmaker because their dad and grandparents and great-grandparents have been watchmakers. They're going to figure out what it is exactly they want to do that will support our community." Thinking back on her wild adventures, she looks settled, concluded, stable.

She eventually rips into one of her anthems, strumming a stray guitar, cast still on her wrist: "Run into my lady friend, she's changed her name again. Leave the city and head down South, we're without purpose. Summer ramblin', we don't know where we're going, but signs we keep pulling to get there."

I lie on the floor and listen, listen, listen. I try to forget about what time it is, how late it is. I trust in the music, in the tenor of her voice, in her kept beat. The kids scream downstairs and Maray's music lulls me. Kitra remains downstairs, snapping photos. For the first time, I feel like I'm getting the hang of the traveling journalist lifestyle, like I am coping, adapting, fitting in—even making friends.

CHAPTER 6

‖‖‖‖‖‖‖‖‖‖‖‖‖‖‖‖‖

The House of Ill Repute

(AUGUST 2010)

WE APPROACH A porch of sour pierced faces. Swallowing my jangled nerves, I smile, then cease smiling immediately, unsure of what to do with my face. A boy with a compass tattooed on his face lies upside down, unconscious, his north arrow pointing downward. The House of Ill Repute, our new home for the week, is a rotted, sagging structure, an itching punk house sunk in the outskirts of Ann Arbor, Michigan. The Meat Mansion, a sister punk house, is located right next door to THOIR. Their adjoining yards are a mash of empty forties, discarded bikes, busted furniture, and wagging, yelping mutts. And, of course, the kids—underage, pierced, shrieking punk kids—are everywhere. Wealthy citizens power walk down this block.

"Hey guys," Maray says, spotting us as we approach. "They're fine," she tells the porch of faces.

We're here because THOIR is Maray Fuego's current place of residence, and she's invited us to stay with her. It's only been a few weeks since New York, and now we're in town for Punk Week, an annual gathering that draws upward of 1,500 buskers, punkers, and rail riders to Ann Arbor. We're here to take more photos and interview more travelers, to document how travelers live together in cities. Like the Rainbow Festival, Punk Week is entirely free, from start to finish. All activities are DIY, with an ethos of anarchism/anti-capitalism. Unlike at Rainbow, you need a connection if you want a place to stay, though many kids sleep outside, in parks, under bridges. Cops troll the streets in August, expecting this annual swell of transients, most of whom are under twenty-five.

Maray welcomes us warmly into her home. Inside, an American flag hangs on the wall, upside down, with an anarchy symbol and slogan penned across it in black Sharpie: YOU SHOULD NOT HAVE TO FEAR YOUR GOVERNMENT YOUR GOVERNMENT SHOULD FEAR YOU. (This is paraphrased from *V for Vendetta*, the dystopian, post-apocalyptic graphic novel by Alan Moore, illustrated by David Lloyd). She leads us up a slanting staircase to an overstuffed attic. It's midsummer and the heat hangs heavy. Halloween decorations from the previous fall hang helter-skelter: cartoon Frankenstein's monsters leering with torn purple eyes, tampons dangling from roof rafters like cotton piñatas. The attic lightbulb is burnt out, so it's hard to see well, but I can make out a wheezing shape in the corner of the hall.

"That's Dumpster Head," Maray says, "my little doggie." The wheezing mutt looks up and coughs. "You can sleep up here tonight," she says, pointing to the floor.

An ominous six-foot-long structure gurgles in the corner. It looks like a small plastic coffin.

"What *is* that?" I ask, perplexed, inspecting.

"Alligator," Maray says, unfazed. "My roommate, Paige, got it at an exotic pet show." She turns and runs back down the creaking stairs.

For any young traveler, punk houses are a staple. They are the places of rest and party between periods of travel, somewhat accessible shelter you can usually count on when traveling through a state. I inspect the rest of the house, curious. In the living room, dirty kids litter the floor like fallen houseflies. I'm overwhelmed by the stench of humans and animals, both reeking of travel. The smell of moving bodies can become bizarrely comforting after a while, like the smell of urination after a night of heavy drinking, that tangy scent that reminds you that you survived the night before, that you're still alive. There is one room in the house devoted exclusively to pets. I enter it warily. Under neon lights sit cages, so many cages, all littered with stinking excrement. White rats scramble in cages; fish slosh in dirty bowls, algae and mold so thick on the glass I can barely see inside; critters yelp and hump everywhere. The utter stench is undeniable. I know the kids care about their dogs, but they can't seem to keep their cages clean.

I leave the room and head outside for air. On the front porch sits a thin girl with face tattoos. She holds a pet crow on her arm. The crow's name is Merlin. The girl has a black boyfriend with dreadlocks who goes by the name SpongeBob, and everyone hates him, though they never say why. Like in Rainbowland, the absence of any people of color in the punk house is obvious and feels somewhat sinister. The girl has clipped Merlin's wings so that he can't fly away, but he flaps and squawks incessantly, like a busted toy plane. Beside them, Cricket, one of the regular THOIR inhabitants, a large man with a bright-blue Mohawk, sits turning the knobs of an oversized boom box, which blasts loud "hot jams," the travelers' name for popular music.

That night, I lie on the floor beside the gator coffin-tank. Kitra is asleep and I'm restless, anxious, seeing shapes in the darkness. I'm wrapped in a silver space blanket I bought at the dollar store, itching and twitching on the filthy beige carpet. I can hear the alligator shifting in the dark beside me, uncomfortable inside those tight walls.

"This is absolute fucking bullshit!" a voice screeches from a bedroom at the other end of the hall. "There are fucking condoms all over my dresser and my floor! There are some random squatter kids sleeping outside my fucking front door!"

The voice belongs to Paige, Maray's housemate, the owner of the alligator. She has just returned from a month or so of travel and is absolutely hysterical. Unfortunately, Kitra and I are those random squatter kids. A male voice, which I take to belong to her boyfriend, soothes her. Within minutes, a new rage—moans and yelps of ecstasy—begins. Listening to this intimate encounter, I suddenly understand why so many kids opt to sleep outside.

A raspy voice penetrates from under the floorboards beneath me.

"So, we found the kid who raped Jen, back in Florida. We fucked him up bad, smashed his fucking jaw!"

I will later learn that the voice belongs to Cricket. I don't know who Jen is, but I feel both frightened and bizarrely comforted to know she is being defended so violently. So often in Babylon, sexual abuse is swept under the rug, ignored entirely.

I don't sleep. I tell myself I am safe, I am fine, I can do this. But I know I'm not safe, not really, that I'm not fine, not really, and that I'm really not sure how much longer I *can* do this.

IN THE MORNING, I have raised bumps on my legs from fleas and bugs, and bags under my eyes. Kitra tells me she slept on a thumbtack. I ask why she didn't say anything.

"I thought it might upset you," she explains, shrugging.

We descend the stairs, step over passed-out kids, mushed cigarette butts, and spilled beers. Both exhausted, we decide to nap for an hour in the park. Kitra and I bundle our packs on a bench. Outside, feeling safer, I drift off to sleep. Moms keep their children at a safe distance, calling them back when they get too close to us. Kids play around our slumbering bodies, and I can't even muster up the energy to feel self-conscious. I change my underwear in the public bathroom and brush my teeth in the drinking fountain. Around the block sits a picked-through garbage can, surrounded by flies. Punk Week participants rummage through old wrappers for meals. When offered, I eat some, too.

Sleep. Glorious sleep. It becomes that thing you lust after on the road, the thing you most miss, the thing you learn how to do everywhere, under or on anything, but never quite reach. You learn how to function on very little of it, how to do it all day, how to live with or without it. The first few days lacking it you feel stoned, then you feel sick, then you feel crazy if it goes too long. The body will sleep anywhere if it's tired enough.

Later in the day, a middle-aged jogger stops to talk to me in the park.

"Do you know when these people will be leaving the park?" he asks me, and I tell him I don't. I wonder why he doesn't think I'm one of them.

"Oh, I'm fine with them," he assures me, after noticing my confused look. His shirt is soaked from navel to nipples in clean, healthy sweat. "It's the dogs I get worried about. It's not an overreaction. I work in an ER. You don't know what a pit bull can do to a child's face."

The relationship between pet and traveler is intrinsic, important, and sacred. Pets are one of the elements of nomadic culture that sedentary folks have the most trouble with. THOIR has a rotating cast of pets: Gore Gore and Noonan. Merlin and Dumpster Head. Actual canine road dogs often hold equal status to their human counterparts. Dogs are a source of warmth, companionship, and protection. I've overheard many homebound folks insist that although they're fine with homeless kids, they have a hard time with the way these people "treat their animals." The irony is that most of those animals, at least the dogs, are some of the most loved pets around—not all, but many. The double irony is that many humans seem to care more about homeless kids' animals than the homeless kids themselves.

TWO HOURS LATER, I find Becky, one of the matriarchs of THOIR. I've noticed she is well respected and in charge of a lot of the cooking. I ask to interview her and she takes me to a couch in the basement of the Meat Mansion.

"He was there when I left last night," Becky tells me, pointing to a teenager passed out beside us on the couch, his drool sticking to the cushion like a string of tape.

Becky has bleached hair and a kind, maternal vibe. She tells me that one of her main concerns about the traveling scene is the trustafarians, who travel just for the summer, "blowing up the culture" for the kids who do it year round out of necessity. She explains that these kids, because of their privilege, don't have to be polite or considerate in their traveling, that they ruin it for the travelers who have no other choice but to travel.

"I'm twenty-seven," she tells me. "I started traveling when I was twenty. I'm kind of settled down now. I guess I've just been traveling slower and slower... When I first started traveling, I had no idea there was this whole subculture of people who were in their twenties or even younger just traveling by train and hitchhiking. I didn't even know that people still did that until I actually left town with my friend, and the places we went we kept meeting more people. It was an eye-opening experience... But the longer I've been traveling, the more it's like, you know— locals... get infatuated with what we're doing, living outside of society, and then they're like, 'Oh, I want to do that. I'm going to do it for the summer.' And, um, I don't know, it kind of irks me, but I guess I just gotta get used to it..."

I ask her why this bothers her—if it's a matter of commitment.

"Well, when I first started traveling, I had no job and no house, and my friend had also no job, but she still had a house. I was living in her basement room on her floor, and she was like, 'Fuck this, let's just get out of here.' And so we left, and had no place to come back to, really. I still have parents in New Mexico, but I couldn't live with them. So I traveled more out of necessity—like, you know, no place to go. And there's no point in wasting away in one place, living until you die. So I went out and had some life experiences."

Upstairs, Maray tells me Pyro, the kid with the compass tattoo on his face, has been committed to a psychiatric ward. I feel shaken. Last night, he fell asleep outside beside a vw that was set on fire. I'm not sure why he was blamed for this fire if he was asleep—the details are murky—but I'm not surprised. Since traveling, I have noticed the police stare at me with suspicious eyes every time I pass by with a pack. I have heard horror stories daily about false accusations, of abuse by authorities.

Kitra and I head out to get lunch and buy groceries, using some of the funds we raised online. Outside the grocery store, we run into Pyro. He looks confused, though his compass tattoo is right side up. We ask him what happened and he confirms that he spent the night in a mental hospital.

"Yeah, they gave me some drug, something starting with a *v*. I was able to sneak out, though, when they weren't paying attention." He seems unfazed.

"Hey, can I use your phone?" he asks Kitra, and she hands it to him, saying, "Of course."

"Hi, Pop. Yeah, I'm in Michigan. How's Mom? That's good, that's good..."

He returns the cell when he's finished and walks off down the street. Feeling off-kilter after the interaction, we walk back to the house.

Back at THOIR, Paige is freaking out. Her turtle has run away. She left him in the care of the house when she was traveling and apparently he has made a break for it. She's inconsolable, pissed

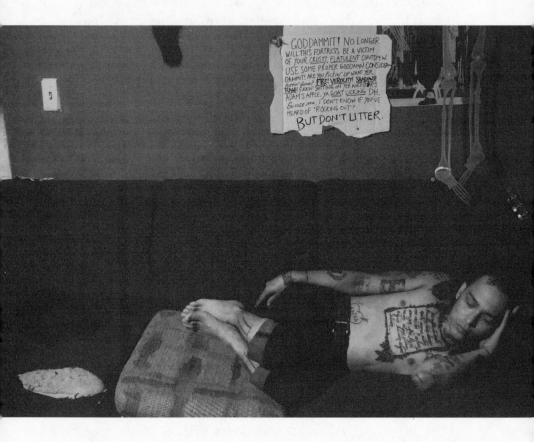

Soup catches up on sleep underneath the house rules at the House of Ill Repute.

MICHIGAN, AUGUST 2010

that nobody looked after her pet properly. She hangs a large, colorful cardboard sign reading *Lost: Tortoise. Have you seen me?* with a cartoon photo drawn below.

I need to caffeinate, to eat, to calm down a little. At the corner store across the street from THOIR I meet Scott, one of the inhabitants I haven't encountered yet. He offers to pay for my iced tea tall can with his food stamps card so that he can nab my dollar. I want to interview him, so he takes me to the Meat Mansion, to where Becky and I sat earlier. His eyes are swirling. Someone told me to stay away from travelers whose eyes spin in a certain direction, but now I can't remember if it's left or right. Scott's speaking and I have a microphone in my hand, so I shove my feelings down. He takes out a tub of strawberry ice cream and slurps the pink goo from a plastic spoon, speaking eloquently about why he travels.

"Freight train riding is the last American endeavor. Everybody feels like there is some freedom that is loosely based upon traveling. I do travel for the freedom. A couple years ago I would be lucky if I went into a town and met one person that was a freight rider… Now, if I go into a [rail] yard, you know, you're going to see a huge place, it's going to be covered in trash [from travelers].

"There was a girl—whose name I'm not going to mention—but she had died, she had died getting on a freight train, she was hit by an Amtrak. There was a little tunnel where everybody used to sit in California, and we would hop out right there. 'Cause she was drunk, she got on it, she died, she got hit by an Amtrak. Now, situations like this make it more difficult for people like myself to get in and out of the yard, harder for us to get on trains, harder for us to make our ends. A lot of travelers fly signs and busk and panhandle. Take an example like this: Punk Week in Ann Arbor. You've got about 1,500 of these young kids—not that they're bad kids, but you have 1,500 of them—and they all got guitars, they all got ukuleles, they all got mandolins, and they're all going to go downtown, and they're all going to do the same thing. Which is going to drain the money from the local community, and it's going to make it more difficult for individuals like myself to go into that community and ask for money, whether it be flying a sign, busking, what have you—you know?"

Scott continues like he's reading from a book. He needs few prompts, as it's clear he has something to say.

"I know this guy, he's an old FTRA guy, and he said: 'Nowadays you guys call them "oogles," the new kids, the kids that are just fresh off the boat. Back in the day, if they came into our jungle, outside of our freight yard, we'd smash their skull in. And that's how we cut such a tight-knit group of people to keep on carrying on the tradition. Now, it's just anybody who feels like they can get on a freight train, well, they just get on it. A lot of people get hurt doing this, a lot of people get messed up doing this. You know, a lot of them are complete stone-cold alcoholic pieces of shit.'"

The Freight Train Riders of America (FTRA) are a notorious collective of homeless tramps and hobos who are often linked to dangerous crimes. William Vollmann's classic text *Riding Toward Everywhere* examines this population. Although I appreciate Vollmann's first-person narrative, his work focuses almost exclusively on male travelers, overlooking other groups and cultures, such as traveling and homeless women and queer street kids—the folks I've been encountering on my travels. Times are changing, and so are the faces of those riding the rails.

Scott, visibly angry, attempts to calm himself down. He slurps another spoon of ice cream and breathes.

"And you know, like anything, there are going to be a group of kids who are going to have to carry on the tradition. But I feel like this culture is just expanding, expanding, expanding, expanding, and—no offense to yourself—but there are a great deal of people who are now documenting it. Not that it hasn't been documented in the past, but now everybody wants to do a documentary on it. I know that as soon as the yardmaster at the freight yard sees this, he's going to be, 'Oh, this is where they've been hopping out,' you know what I mean? With all due respect."

I ask Scott if he finds that drinking and drugs are a huge problem in the traveling scene.

"I mean, when you're on the streets, dude, it can suck. I don't know if you realize this, but sometimes you're just out there and there's no shelter anywhere, you're in the middle of, like, Interstate 80 going across the country hitchhiking, and rainclouds, they just form, and they pour, and they don't stop, you know, for two days. Everything you own is completely soaked. You can't hitchhike, you ain't got no food, you ain't got no beer, nothing. People don't understand that about people that travel, they don't understand how difficult it can be. And I think that—I was a heroin addict for ten years—you know, I think that plays a large role in why people drink so much and why people do so many drugs. Because when you get into situations like that, after a while you haven't seen a home. I mean, I haven't seen my sister in seven years and she lives in Michigan, okay? I haven't seen my mom in four and a half years, and that's the only family I got. I haven't seen them in years, and some of these kids out here haven't seen their family in longer. They're just out there on the road and they get that ten-thousand-mile stare, and sometimes it's just really, really weird and awkward, and really hard to cope with these problems."

I clutch my microphone tighter, even more nervous, but press on, reminding myself not to be afraid. And I'm not afraid of Scott, even when he begins to explain what he means by the ten-thousand-mile stare.

"That's like in Vietnam or travelers, freight riders, that's like when you stare at somebody you're not staring at them, you're staring behind them, you're staring through them, you're staring around them. Like when you're in a freight train yard, and some-one's talking to you, and you're like, 'Yeah, I hear ya,' really what you're paying attention to is that that freight train's moving. Or if you're on a road and you see headlights, and you've got your thumb out—whether or not you can dictate whether that car's coming your way or whether that car's pulled over and parked. Or if you're in a very shady situation, where you're surrounded by people that you might not know, you're, like, looking off in the corner, staring at his friend while you're talking to this guy who's very angry at you, you know what I mean? It's like... it's staring further. You don't really look at people anymore. You look beyond them. It's weird. You know, that terminology comes from Viet-nam actually, because a lot of freight riders came back from Vietnam, they didn't have a home, they didn't have nowhere, Mom died or whatever, buddy Johnny stepped on a land mine. You know, and the terminology rolled over into the hobo com-munity, because a lot of the old hobos from the seventies, a lot of the old heads now, they all had that ten-thousand-mile stare...

"You take people and you put them on the track, twenty years, I mean hard traveling, like, like get on that fucking train and you fucking go, do that for twenty years. You got no family, all your friends are tramps or hobos, you know, or hippies that stay at Gatherings, you know, that's all you know, that's outside of soci-ety. You take that individual after twenty years of fucking long hauls and close calls, and you just take that son of a bitch and you put him in a nice clean pair of khakis and maybe a button-up shirt, and you take this individual and you put him into a store and tell him to get a goddammed job. He can't! He doesn't know how to live like that."

Scott offers me a high five and we smack palms. I thank him for his wisdom and he makes a wet farting noise with his mouth. When I ask him for any advice on where to travel next, he tells me, without doubt, that I should go to New Orleans.

"Everyone goes through New Orleans," he says. "Everybody."

"A crazy scene?" I ask.

"An interesting scene."

His eyes stop spinning. He finishes the dregs of his strawberry ice cream and licks the plastic container clean.

TODAY IS THE day Dumpster Head loses his balls. We're sitting on the porch waiting for the van to go to the vet. Josh, Maray's boyfriend, drives up and we all pile in. There are no seats, so we jockey for position in the back, balancing on hard metal, listening to jazz on the radio. The vet's office is in the swanky part of Ann Arbor, with clean facades and trimmed grass. Everyone inside the clinic is well groomed. Josh sits beside me in a laminate chair: dirty hands, hand-poked tattoos, no shoes. The other patrons have the usual pets: golden retrievers, Siamese cats, birds— though only the exotic kind, no ravens, no seagulls, no crows.

"Hey, whatever happened to Merlin?" I ask Josh. "I haven't seen him around in a few days."

"That crow?"

"Yeah."

"Merlin's dead, dude."

I am shocked. "How? When?"

"SpongeBob sat on him."

Josh and I begin to laugh nervously, then a little louder, with a mix of horror and titillation. We just laugh and laugh, and that's the end of it. What else can we do? Merlin is dead.

Dumpster Head bounds through the vet's doors, ball-less. A weary-looking nurse in a mauve uniform follows him. I wonder who paid for the operation and assume Maray did. She has been doing odd jobs locally and must have saved up the cash. Her friends are here for moral support.

"You have to make sure he doesn't bite at his stitches," the nurse tells Maray, who nods her shaved head in compliance.

"This is very important. He will get infected. You might want to buy him a cone."

"Aren't there any herbal remedies I can use?" Maray asks.

"No," the nurse says shortly. "Absolutely not."

On the car ride home, DH is hazy, bumping into the passengers in the seatless back, woozy on four legs. He rests his deflated ball sack on a stray sneaker in the back of the truck, a futile attempt to find comfort. Maray cuddles him, seeming regretful of her decision, not knowing if she made the right choice, not sure of herself at all.

"I definitely don't want to be a mother," she had told me a few days earlier. "I can barely look after a dog."

Josh brings us to his home in the woods across the tracks from the punk houses. He leads us across the tracks, up through the foliage, brushing back prickly bushes and oak branches, following a loose path. The woods are located behind a black fraternity house, but Josh insists they're cool with him passing through their yard to get to his fort.

"A whole community lives in these woods at night," he says. "They clean up their forts every night, so they don't get evicted."

We walk past an encampment built into the woods below the Ann Arbor graveyard. It looks like a human-made beaver lodge, with tarps and discarded bed sheets. Josh's home is fairly small, one bedroom, made entirely from found scraps of wood and materials.

Back at THOIR I ask him what he thinks about traveling culture, and he talks to me openly and quickly. We're lounging up in Maray's room.

"I idolize and, like—not idolize, but fantasize and romanticize—moving around a lot and waking up in a different place as much as possible, just because it naturally keeps you invigorated, because you have to be in order to be constantly creative in a new environment as opposed to being habitual and repetitive and patterned out when you are in one place."

His statements and air remind me of a quotation I read in an academic paper by Nial Anderson entitled "A Study into Hobo Literature": "The emotional strength of the hobo is a liberating concept, that a person needn't be controlled by society or sometimes even his bodily needs." I wonder if one of the appeals of traveling is that it forces you, sometimes, to be fully present, to appreciate what is in front of you, to live life moment to moment. In his *Autobiography of a Super-Tramp*, W.H. Davies speaks to this idea: "When I suffered most from lack of rest, or bodily sustenance—as my actual experience became darker, the thoughts of the future became brighter, as the stars shine to correspond with the night's shade."

Someone changed the lightbulb in the attic room, and I get a good look at Paige's gator. I peek over the edge of the plastic coffin, hesitant, on guard. The creature cowers back, pupils dilating at the sight of my dark figure. She isn't very big, about a forearm long, with brown plaid skin and swirling yellow rings around her eyes. She looks hungry, or maybe scared; I can't tell which and know sometimes they're the same thing. Her slick head shakes at me, trying to evaluate whether I'm a threat. I can't offer her answers; I just stare. The gator pushes her rump against the plastic wall behind her for comfort, to remind herself that she is home, that she is safe. I don't like the look of her, crammed tight in the plastic coffin, trapped inside. Paige told me she bought her at an exotic pet show, and I wonder if she was raised inside or captured from the wild. Something about her eyes makes me feel nauseous, so I turn and run down the attic stairs, back outside. I'm beginning to question the kids' ability to care for their creatures entirely.

"HEY! SHUT THE FUCK UP!" someone screeches. "We're getting started."

Outside, kids gather in the HOIR field; some sit in busted wheelchairs, some on molding lawn chairs, most on the mud.

Kitra and I join the crew to nods, hugs, and a line of new faces, always new faces. The cursing and yelling calms down as kids take swigs from shared forties and smoke hand-rolled cigarettes. At the center of the yard sits a schedule board, laying out the Punk Week activities. Tasks are read out, assigned, and quickly passed down the line. Names are written sloppily in thick black Sharpie on the tattered board. Progress is made impressively quickly.

"Who's in charge of the zombie walk, and where are we starting from?"

Before the zombie march, I cover my face with white talcum powder, draw a black crucifix in the center of my forehead, and dribble a bit of colored corn-syrup blood down the side of my mouth; it tastes cheap and sweet. Kids are in good spirits, jovial, slapping backs, dressing up. Vulture is filling his mouth with the stuff, spitting it onto friends and fellow zombies. Lots of the kids have dressed up their pets as well, covered them in syrup, drawn scars and masks onto their furry faces, dyed them green. We are called to assemble by a blonde woman, who I've pieced together is the mother of the green-faced, blonde-haired child running around the field.

"We are not trying to get the cops called, we are not in a cop versus punk war. We are going to try and do something like, hey look what those punk kids are doing, it's pretty cool. We're not fucking shit up... It isn't about getting the goddamn cops called on you, it isn't about fucking up Ann Arbor because you're not from here. This is for the people that love this town, we're doing this as something for all of us to get together and have a good time with, so don't fuck it up for everybody else. Let's all go have a good time."

The crowd explodes in claps.

We are led by a zombie band, complete with cymbals, marching band drums, trumpets, and trombones. The zombies keep a stagnant off-key beat for us to march to, and we do, flailing, lopsided, snarling, undead. Babylonians pull out iPhones and cameras to film us, mostly friendly and supportive. We walk into the core of Ann Arbor, where the mood is less relaxed. An elderly woman walking a dog crosses the street to pass through the zombie procession. She has a stern, unimpressed pout. She walks directly up to me as I pull the most dazed, semi-ferocious zombie face I can muster.

"You are disgusting!" she screams, directly into my face, with so much spite and determination I am actually taken aback. I think back to Monique in New York, being yelled at in her see-through panties and bra. "Look at the mess you are making! Look at your animals. You are disgusting!"

Kids look at her blankly, some cracking smiles, others revealing no expression whatsoever. She is seething. To her, I am not some outsider taking notes; I am a full-fledged player, a runaway scumbag. She has no idea where I come from, what my backstory is. All she sees is something dirty and dangerous that she wishes wasn't there. For one split second, I feel that true hatred that so many kids experience on a daily basis. I feel what it is like to be seen as a genuine monster. I croak out my best zombie groan back into her old face and keep on moving.

Later, I contemplate the exchange. Where did her anger come from? Was she afraid of me? Was she upset at travelers altogether? The more I travel the more I notice the odd interactions between travelers and stationary Babylonians. Oftentimes, the traveler becomes a poster child for all those pent-up fears that keep sedentary citizens sedentary: fear of dirt, fear of sexuality, fear of death and insanity—the fears that keep them homebound. Instead of people or kids, they see drunk hobos, whores, and drug addicts. The more I move, the less I worry about what these standstill people call me. The road strips you down. It makes you calloused. It makes you infinitely independent. It makes you dirty, and it makes you free.

In *Anarchy in the Age of Dinosaurs*, an anarchist collective manifesto, rebellion is linked inextricably to travel: "Some naysayers will argue that travel is not radical, in and of itself. And this is true: a millionaire can jump on an airplane to Barbados and have an entire hotel to himself, just as a crustie in the U.S. can ride trains motivated solely by cheap escapism. The potential of travel lies in its relative freedoms: time to dedicate to projects, the ability to convey materials and information, flexibility in putting energy into new projects, supporting faraway comrades, the list continues on. Travel can also be used to combat isolation and to give us hope in an otherwise unwelcoming world. As any traveler knows, getting somewhere you've never been requires patience and dedication."

As we round the streets of downtown Ann Arbor, we head for a park. Word circulates that the cops are on their way. We decide to change our route to avoid police intervention. Cricket and his friend Sam have showed up with canisters filled with fake blood, which they are squirting maniacally. The mood becomes a little more aggressive. The kids have started their "planned attacks," in which they jump upon "non-zombies," usually friends of theirs they have planted. The procession leads back to the river, a standby spot for traveling punk kids.

When we reach the river, many of the zombies jump right in, blood and face paint melting from their hot pores, creating pools of grease in the water. Slowly, their makeup is stripped off, but the kids look funny on the banks, half-covered in zombie makeup, half-clean. I realize there's not so much of a difference between the dress-up and their everyday. Travelers are used to people staring at them, gawking, horror-eyed. Once a year, they are allowed to gawk back, eyes blank, blood-covered. *Look at your jobs, your storefronts,* they are saying. *Look at your everyday life. Are we the zombies?* Half of me feels invigorated to be part of the community, included by virtue of discrimination by the public, but the other part feels afraid.

Pyro shows off his compass face tattoo.
MICHIGAN, AUGUST 2010 ·

A DAY LATER, kids pile into cars and travel to a barn on the outskirts of the city. Outside, a large mud pit has been built and dirty, wormy bodies are writhing within.

"Hit her knees!" Vulture screams from the sidelines at Janessa. She lunges at her opponent. Janessa and Vulture arrived in their van, pit bull in tow. I haven't seen them since New York.

All the men are wearing dresses. We're at Burly Girl Mud Wrestling, with a hundred or so road kids cooking corn and slinging mud. Unlike in mainstream mud wrestling, there is nothing sexual about these fights. A girl named Jess with cupcake tattoos and butt-length dreadlocks has been paired with Janessa. As the girls collide into each other there is a split second of silence before they drop—*splat*—into the mud. The sound is like a spanking, a vicious thud. The onlookers cheer and gasp, and are slapped in the face with specks of mud and water and sweat.

"My girl is tough! She is one of the best fighters I've ever seen!" Vulture yelps on the sidelines, impressed, his dog yelping along.

As the crowd grows, a girl organizing the event grabs a megaphone and tells everyone to assemble around the pit—a huge pen made from planks of wood filled to the top with thick, luscious mud. A man named Soup sits on the sidelines, chugging water from an old jug. Meanwhile, Cricket, wearing a blond wig over his blue Mohawk, runs a makeshift bar out of the red barn beside the pit. He's wasted already, and kids line up out the barn door.

Cheers flood the field as the two fighters try to regain their footing. The mud is extremely thick, which makes the women move in slow motion, glue on their joints. They put up a good fight for about three minutes, but eventually Jess is victorious. She smacks her opponent facedown in the mud, suffocating her, and wins the first round.

I hear a rumor there is a hep C wrestling round, once everyone has finished, for those with the blood-borne illness. Infection travels rapidly in dirt and water.

"That's very responsible of them," Kitra notes when my jaw drops.

I remember Becky had told me how easy and common it is for kids to get hep C through partners or sharing needles. Since symptoms are often mild, kids don't even know they've been infected. Needles have always freaked me out.

"You may be sitting under a bridge because you're going to sleep there that night and, oops, you get stuck with a dirty rig and, hey, you've got AIDS. This stuff happens," she told me.

An hour into the fight, we are interrupted by the sound of two dogs getting in a jaw-snapping brawl. One of the dogs is the pit bull belonging to Vulture and Janessa. Seeing the dangerous fight, Vulture grabs his dog, tackling it to the ground.

"Bad dog!" he screeches, slapping it across the face. "Bad dog!"

"What the fuck are you doing?" a local from the crowd demands angrily. She gets up in Vulture's face, shouting. I can tell by her dress and cleanliness that she is not a traveling kid but a local hipster. "You can't treat an animal like that!"

This exchange provokes a huge screaming match between the two sides, travelers and non-travelers, and the crowd separates suddenly. The kids seem to think physical abuse is appropriate— necessary, even—and the other onlookers deem it cruel.

"This is a fighting dog. It used to be a fighter. You have to train it like this. This is how it learns," Vulture responds, shocked and hurt. There is no question that the dog means the world to him.

"I don't care. That's not how you treat an animal!" she screams, and leaves.

Vulture's friends console him. "Fuck that hippie, man. You did the right thing." He is visibly shaken.

Burly Girl resumes with a new pair of women. The slosh of mud and grunts wear on and I get tired. I stand farther from the pit as I notice my clothes growing a brown coat. Soup sits by the fire, dressed in a spotless shirt and a fedora, smoking a cigarette, somehow still clean. He is gorgeous. Looking down at my muddy body, I notice a strange discoloration on my chest, white dots on my beige skin, which seems to be spreading. I try to wipe it off, but it stays put. I return to my circle of friends and ask some kids what they think it might be.

"Travelers' fungus."

I don't mud wrestle, afraid of the hep C situation, and spooked by my mutating skin. I am getting tired and hungry, so I ditch the fight and walk to the closest food source—a Burger King a mile down the highway. I need to eat. I need to push down tiredness, fear, an uncomfortable feeling. I order fries and a chocolate milkshake, shoving the junk food down my throat, barely chewing. On the walk home, woozy, I begin seeing stars. The food, crumpled and mashed, comes back up my throat easily. I leave it on the roadside and keep moving.

When I return to Burly Girls, the light is failing and there is a line of cop cars blinking outside the barn. *Shit.* Returning to the yard, I find Josh sunk in a chair, deflated.

"What happened?"

"Cops arrested a bunch of the kids earlier, down by the river. Now they're here."

"What were they doing at the river that got them arrested?"

"Skinny-dipping. Eating chicken."

It seems strange that the kids would be arrested for eating chicken and skinny-dipping, but Sal confirms it. He is livid. We had lent him a recorder earlier that week to record his friends' bands, and he used it to record the cops—cops who shouted at a group of dirty kids, calling them "faggots" and "niggers," dragging them screaming into police cars. I am disgusted—aghast. We hitch a ride back into Ann Arbor and plan to visit the jail in the morning.

IN THE MORNING, at the jail, Babylonians are staring and the guards eyeball us. We approach the building with a pack of fellow travelers and meet more inside. We are forced to check all our belongings in a locker. They check our shoes and hats. They don't admit our camera or recorder. They give us sneers, angry looks, irritation. Inside, we find no help. The police tell us the kids have been transferred to another facility, but they won't tell us where. They also won't tell us what the charges are, or when we can expect the kids to get out. Eventually they send us home and tell us to return in the morning.

Back at THOIR the mood is still jovial. I'm struck by how unaffected the punks appear, but I'm getting used to this constant indifference. A handsome man named Cliff wears brown overalls and no shirt; a tattoo on his breast reads *I Love Patios*. He has been traveling for more than eight years. I introduce myself. He tells me his real name is Clifford Elliot III, but Cliff will do. His charming smile is insistent, his Southern drawl infectious. (We will become fast friends; he and Kitra will become more than that, and quick. Soon, he's following her around like a puppy. They cuddle on the roofs of cars. I miss that sort of affection, and feel a pang of jealousy.)

Cliff is a bike punk, a popular subset of punk traveling culture. He is biking across the country with nothing but his wheels, a pack, and a washboard for busking. He has stopped in Ann Arbor for Punk Week, to meet up with old friends. I'm not sure whom he knows at the House of Ill Repute, but that's usually the case with the kids who show up. There's something intensely calming about Cliff, about his overall friendliness, his buoyancy.

We head to Maray's room so that I can interview him about his past, about how he started traveling. He stares at my dirty face, distracted.

"Can I pop your zit?" he asks me.

"Um, okay," I concede as he puts his paws on my cheek, squeezes his fingers around the yellow bulge. He applies pressure and the zit pops.

"Yeah, got it!" he shrieks, excitedly, and we begin the interview.

"Okay, it all kinda started when I was thirteen... I actually used to want to be a kindergarten teacher. But, I got into graffiti, caused $6,000 worth of damages to my school, got kicked out of school three months into ninth grade—I was an honor student, but I got kicked out of my school. None of the other schools would take me, because of my reputation for destruction that I caused at the school I was in. My dad couldn't afford homeschooling, so that was the end of my school career. I got a job when I was fifteen. I didn't want to work anymore, so I quit when I was sixteen. Then one day my dad and I got into it and he kicked me out. So I went to downtown Houston—that's where I'm from, Houston, Texas—and I was there for a couple weeks. I met some kids there, one was named Scarecrow and the other was Alex, one twenty-one, the other twenty-four. I was like, 'Oh, I haven't seen you guys around here,' and they said, 'We're just traveling here,' and we got to talking about it and I found out that they hopped freight trains. So I asked them to take me with them. They kept saying no, but I kept on bugging them about it. They went to go leave, so I followed them and jumped on a car a few behind them and rode on my first train with no backpack, no water, no food, which is not a very smart idea when it's 760 miles from Houston, Texas, to El Paso, Texas. So I got off when I saw them get off, and followed them... and they were both like, 'Goddamnit,' and then kinda started to show me some things... And that's how I started traveling."

Cliff tells me he is now educating himself, seeing the world without money, meeting interesting people every day. I ask him if, having seen so much of his country, he feels he has a different sense of the U.S. than most. I ask if he likes his country, if he feels it's a good place.

"I feel like America is just like any other country, it's just, you know, different regions have different styles of people with different morals or ethics, or different stuff they grow up with. The

South is very homey, with big meals, but racist as well, depending on the parts. If you go northeast, they're all hippies or really hardworking guys, all about fashion and whatnot... To me, it's got nothing to do with country—it's the people. People watching, which is pretty fun, you know—how people react to things, what they do in their lives, and what their beliefs are."

The positivity Cliff brings to Ann Arbor is soon tested. The day after our interview, his bike is stolen—his only real possession and sole mode of transportation. He left it on the HOIR lawn among other bikes overnight and somebody snatched it. On top of that, later, while drinking away his sorrows, he breaks his washboard in half and mashes his tailbone doing a dangerous stunt. It seems it is not this Texan's day. I expect, reasonably, for him to lose it. But even drunk, he remains fairly placid and easygoing about life.

"I may have broke my tailbone and lost my bike and got my board smashed up, but I still love life," he tells me, sucking on a tall can.

The streets are flooded. The rain has barfed across the sidewalk, sloshing uncontrollably down the clean streets of the city. The water is muddy and murky. I suspect the sewers have backed up and overflowed. Kids from the Meat Mansion have blown up plastic dinghies and are pulling each other down the road in bubble boats. Cliff has somehow found a bright yellow kayak and is paddling gleefully down the street. Kids are helping rained-in cars vacate parking lots. We run around, getting our feet wet. I've never seen anything like it.

Later, Kitra and I go out for tacos. We run into Bounce, a kid we met earlier that week who had been banned from THOIR, though we were never told why. I've heard vague rumors that he is a skinhead. He weighs about a hundred pounds.

"I just stabbed some home bum!" he shouts at us as he walks by.

"Home bum" is the term for a non-traveling homeless person, like the men who ask for change outside of liquor stores.

When Bounce sees our looks of dumbfounded shock, he adds, "He was trying to rape a prostitute."

Up close we can see his spinning eyes, the tear tattoo. He must be about eighteen years old, max.

"Don't tell the cops you saw me," he says, running away.

We don't.

BACK AT THE house, kids are fixing up bikes.

Kozmo, a scruffy, thin kid, is dressed in orange short shorts and a long, red wig. When we enter he looks angry. He doesn't say hello.

"Why are you doing this book?" he asks. "It has already been done."

He stares me down. My stomach sinks.

"You're a hipster, you should know that. Kitra's not, but you are."

I wonder what it is that separates us. I wonder how he can see through me so clearly. I wonder why sometimes I am let in instantly and other times excluded. All I know is that when I'm questioned, I feel like a parasite, like a bug about to get crushed.

"The Polaroid Kidd took photos of the subculture a few years back. We were good friends. But he sold out."

Mike Brodie—AKA the Polaroid Kidd—wrote a book, *A Period of Juvenile Prosperity,* that had come up during my research. I'd flipped through the pages, astounded. His first-person reportage, his images and writing, had inspired me, and I recognized some of the faces from our own travels. I'm shocked to hear that he's perceived as a "sellout"—through my online correspondence I had found he was working on trains, taking photos, and writing. He certainly wasn't getting wealthy off his images, which made the label more confusing. Was anyone who represented travelers an instant sellout?

I try to make it clear we are genuine, that we actually give a shit about this project, but Kozmo is not buying it. I'm not sure if Kozmo likes us or hates us. I'm not sure he knows.

"Don't blow up the culture," he says.

This isn't the first time I've heard this and it won't be the last. I think back to my interview with Scott in the basement.

As Punk Week progresses, a local documentary crew begins filming some of the activities around THOIR. The kids seem immediately angered by this intrusion, and I am, too. I'm skeptical of stationary outsiders.

"We had a meeting about the documentary crew," Becky tells me. "We decided you and Kitra were fine, but we don't like the other guys. We don't want them interviewing us."

I smile silently, feeling accepted.

A children's aid worker starts stopping by the house, asking the kids, including Kitra and me, about our living situations and offering help. Apparently this is a common occurrence. THOIR is a blight on the neighborhood, packed to the rim with underage kids, and I guess people are starting to take notice. We keep quiet when we're asked questions, not wanting to betray any confidences.

ONE OF THE HOIR kids, Andrea, with a shaved head and thick septum ring, tells us she lives in a tree house a short drive away. We ask to see her home. She obliges happily.

"You can meet Grandpa Don!" she exclaims excitedly.

We hitch out to the forest to see her setup.

Grandpa Don, a man in his mid-seventies, lives in the woods on the outskirts of Ann Arbor. He helps out a bunch of the street kids, getting them work, letting them camp on his land, and lending out his homemade tree houses for them to live in full time. Andrea lives in one of those tree houses.

As we approach her tree house, Andrea seems nervous. "My place is probably a mess," she says shyly, walking barefoot up the highway to her home.

On the side of the road, we find a decaying porcupine, old road-kill. Its teeth are rotting out of its face, prodding upward into the sun, a spiteful grin on its dead face. We walk down a pathway of trees into the Michigan wilderness, until we reach a small brown bungalow with a white-haired man sitting on the porch outside.

"Grandpa Don!" Andrea shouts. "I want you to meet my friends."

Don is a sprightly man—thin, mobile, and quick. He greets us warmly and begins talking to us about nutrition almost instantly.

"I read an article in *Reader's Digest* that says eggs cause breast cancer," he says.

We sit outside and shoot the shit with Don for a while, and he eventually invites us in for a game of space ball.

"What is space ball?" I ask.

Don leads us inside the brown bungalow, where we see that it is not a house but a gymnasium, stacked to the walls with weights, machines, and last (but not least) a number of professional floor-bound trampolines. Don teaches us the rules of space ball.

"The goal of space ball is to score while bouncing on the tramp," he says, pointing to the hoop built into the center net.

He invites Kitra and me to step onto the tramps and get our footing. We get on and instantly start bouncing around, excited to let loose and have fun. After a few minutes, we are huffing and puffing from the exercise.

The next game he shows us, for which we have to use the other trampoline, consists of bouncing over a swinging rod. Turns out Don fell in love with the tramp in college, when he was introduced to the sport and began competing professionally. The goal of his forest setup was to have a commercial gym where people could train on trampolines. Apparently Don's gym isn't getting much business—probably because it is located in the middle of a forest plot outside of Ann Arbor—but he feels confident that business will heat up.

"People love tramps," he tells us, and I can't argue with that.

Andrea decides it's time to show us her home. She leads us up a path from Don's to a small hand-built tree house. Outside sits a tent that she sleeps in half the time. Someone else has been sleeping in the tree house since Andrea has been away traveling. Inside is a collection of treasures and objects, sleeping bags, and tons of survivalist, queer, and feminist zines. She offers us one called *Surviving in the Wilderness* that includes a play-by-play on how to lose government trackers who might be monitoring your life "off the map." (Many nomads live briefly with communes and co-ops across the country. Survivalism is popular in these self-sufficient spaces.) Andrea tells us that although she loves living at Don's, her plan is to move out to Asheville, North Carolina, to live in a commune she once visited.

She's twenty-seven, but she could easily pass for a teenager. She tells us that she needs to get out of Ann Arbor, away from her dysfunctional family. She shows us around the rest of the lot, pausing to explain the origins and names of almost every plant she finds. Her knowledge of botany is impressive. She tells us to watch for poison ivy.

She leads us to another tree house, currently empty, which is usually occupied by another transient family with a child. It is even more complex than Andrea's, with bunk beds and a desk lamp. The construction is impressive.

"Grandpa Don built these all himself," she tells us.

Andrea invites us to spend the night in her tent outside, and I welcome the idea. The idea of staying in a tent is a luxury after the punk houses we've been sleeping in. We spread out our sleeping bags and soak in the silence all around us. It is quiet, still, save for the bugs chirping. It is nice to feel outside, closer to nature, safe.

AFTER WAKING UP in our tent, we head back to THOIR. Elanor, the young girl with dreads and a busted accordion we met back in New Mexico, is outside, playing music. She lives up the street from THOIR in a nice, small one-story house with her family. Her mother is a leading raw food chef in Michigan, but she's away, so the kids have taken over, cooking meat, slicing cheese on counters, misbehaving. A girl named Carrie is there with a thick black eye. She tells us she fell down the stairs at THOIR and busted it up, her face shining like a shot-up tin can. We sit around with four huge dogs jumping with fleas. A naked blond child runs around the house. Carrie slaps her dog for stealing a piece of chicken off her plate. *Freaks*, a 1932 film about circus sideshow performers, plays on the TV. It features real deformed humans—men with pinheads, Siamese twins—and the kids stare, transfixed. Kitra falls asleep in the corner instantly and I'm left watching. Even though I'm under the safe cover of a roof, I don't feel any less anxious. Elanor brings me a few blankets and I wrap them around myself, pushing dogs off me when they try to nuzzle in. I drift off to sleep with the film playing in the background, fleas chomping on my shins.

"One of us!" the main freak shouts at a woman, holding a chicken drumstick. "One of us!"

CHAPTER 7

On Fire

(AUGUST 2010)

B Y THE TIME I reach Detroit, I've had a pit stop in Vancouver: enough time to do laundry, try to sleep off the stress, then fly back to Michigan. Incessant travel is getting to me. I do not feel golden.

I spend my first night in Detroit near the university, alone on the couch of a girl I met online. Her name is Ryan. I found her on Couchsurfing.com, a site that links up travelers with free places to sleep. Although it's often used as a dating service, full-time travelers and weekend warriors alike also frequent it. Ryan keeps a snake in a small cage beside her couch, which hisses all night.

"It's feeding day," she tells me in the morning, dangling four live mice by their tails above the serpent's jaws.

I watch each mouse perform a uniquely pitiful struggle before the black jaw clamps down. I wonder where Ryan buys these feeder mice, how much each one costs, how pet stores decide which mice to sell as pets and which for food. Outside, Detroit looks like a piece of gray Swiss cheese: holey and half-empty. Space takes up more room than the substance holding it together. Crumpling concrete is everywhere. It is a bizarre, haunting city:

a fallen Rome, past home of the auto industry, city of Ford and Pontiac.

I am in the city for a celebration at the Crow Manor called the Crownival, which kids from THOIR and the Meat Mansion are attending. Kitra and I are reuniting after a week apart. We've both been traveling a lot, but I am feeling the strain more: I'm snappy, dizzy, and emotional.

On the train to Detroit, a pink, puffy police officer chatted me up while I waited for the doors to open. He grimaced after I told him where I was headed.

"*Why* would you want to go to Detroit?" he asked incredulously.

"Why not?" I responded, confused, quickly boiling up. My experiences in the activist scene, and now traveling, had only intensified my absolute mistrust of police, which is ever evolving into disgust the more I have to deal with them.

"It's awful *ghetto* there, if you know what I mean," the man continued, chuckling. "I can't say what I'd like to say, because I'm on duty, but I'm sure you can read between the lines." He winks and I squint my eyes, wincing.

Walking alone in downtown Detroit, I'm approached by a group of four young black men. As they pass, one mutters to me, reassuringly, "Don't worry, there's nothing to be afraid of."

The comment hangs in my mind like a wet sheet. Had I looked afraid?

I continue to the Avalon bakery to meet up with Kitra, who was making her way to Detroit separately. The bakery owner eyes me, looking entertained.

"Where are you from?" he asks.

"Canada," I respond.

"It sure is different here, ain't it?"

I nod, eating as much bread as my body can hold.

Kitra arrives within the hour. We decide to walk to the Crow Manor together, as we don't have any other way to get there. As we start off on foot, two tattooed men dressed as clowns pull up beside us in a rusty pickup truck.

"Hey, pretty ladies! You want a ride?"

The clowns are Cricket and Sam, two kids from THOIR, who are also on their way to the Crownival. I jump in and sit shotgun, and Kitra takes the back. Lady, a caramel-colored pit bull, yelps as we pull onto the road. I see Kitra's lanky legs flailing in the rearview as she almost falls out of the back of the truck onto the pavement.

"Oops! Sorry about that," Cricket slurs, slowing down for a second, then speeding up.

Sam sits in the back, holding a plastic bag of live crickets, which bounce around inside like dirty popcorn.

"They're for the freak show," he explains. "We're going to eat them."

As we pull up to the Crow Manor, we see a stream of punks—travelers, crusties, anarchists, and hybrids—carrying paper bags with bottles peeking out and babies in slings. Plastic carousel ponies are strewn about the yard. The crowd is an eclectic mix of dirty kids, children, and dogs. There are so many dogs, drooling creatures snapping and humping everywhere. The Crow Manor was once a gorgeous Victorian structure, no doubt home to a wealthy family. Now it functions as a collective for artists, musicians, and activists. Inside the house are salvaged traveling signs, lights, instruments, and raggedy couches. There seem to be rooms everywhere, kids everywhere. Residents pass out flyers printed on electric-green paper that give the order of events: *Kissing Booth, Face Painting, Tarot Reading, Kombucha Stand, Free Tattoos, Texas Hold 'Em, Pin the Leg on Fat Patty, Drag Bicycle Race.* There are a bunch of musical acts lined up, including Stumps Duh Clown and Grotesque Burlesque.

A number of kids from THOIR are here, including Josh and Maray. Maray takes us on a tour of the surrounding area of downtown Detroit. We come across a bunch of men standing around a barrel fire, and when we walk by, they look up suspiciously. Maray leads us around the corner and I am confronted with an astounding site: a large-scale urban farm in the middle of the city.

"They burnt down the abandoned buildings to make this place," she explains. "Now we have this farm."

We arrive at a huge squatted complex with an outdoor toilet and shower. Burritos are being sold from a trailer.

"Families live here now."

I'm intrigued by the patches of planted greens, alive amid the concrete chaos and decay.

When we return to Crow Manor, Soup, whom I last saw at Burly Girl in Ann Arbor, is onstage performing a grotesque striptease. He wears a black G-string under fishnets and punctuates his act with smoker's coughs and hocked loogies. He binge-eats chicken wings from a bucket as he reveals his body parts to the jeers and screeches of an inebriated crowd. I watch him, blurry-eyed, spinning, and feel embarrassed by my attraction to him. I'm feeling very lonely and it's beginning to show.

I meet Stevee an hour later at the dumpstered banquet table. She has bugged eyes and parts of her scalp are shaved bare. She's small and attractive, with arms covered in stick and pokes. She tells me it must be nice working and traveling with my best friend, and I tell her yes, it is—but I don't mention my constant anxiety, my vomiting and nausea, my loneliness and fear. I'm working, after all, so I try to keep up appearances. Stevee opens up quickly when I ask to interview her.

"My mother was a scam artist and I was her kid, so we traveled everywhere and stole people's credit cards and lived off of $2,000 spending limits," she confides.

"I've lived in trailers, I've lived with six other people in the same room as a child… I've been left alone for weeks to live on my own, when I was very young. I was sovereign from my parents when I was eleven years old."

She laughs at the strangeness of her life story, looking at her tattooed arms and smoking. I think of my father, my mother, my stability growing up, and I feel parasitic. I ask Stevee if she considers herself to be an American.

"No. I live in New Orleans, it's different. We are sovereign… We eat well, we drink a lot, we work a lot, and we play a lot, and we don't ever quit."

She tells me she works in a kitchen in the city but travels a lot. Then she tells me her mushrooms have just kicked in, so she has to go.

I'm left alone to think. The differences between our lifestyles are so obvious, and I'm curious about how she's become comfortable in chaos when I feel like I'm constantly treading water.

Outside, the jeers of the Crown have heightened. I'm overwhelmed. I feel I should be getting used to my surroundings, having been in them for so long, but I can't adjust. I'm tired and I want to be alone. I leave the Crownival and return to the house where Kitra and I are staying that night—another online find. They've let us pitch a tent in their backyard. I sit in the tent, breathing nervously in the middle of downtown Detroit, listening to gunshots and hollering bodies outside the thin plastic walls. *You are safe. You are okay,* I try. *You are safe. You are okay.* But I know it's a lie.

I call a guy I'm dating in my life back in Vancouver. I'm desperate for comfort. He picks up, off guard.

"You really don't sound okay," he says. "Maybe you're not cut out for this."

"What're you trying to say?" I ask.

"Well, Kitra seems to manage it okay. You just sound horrible."

I feel weak, afraid, incompetent, lost.

"Just come home," he says.

Maray Fuego spits fire during a performance at the Detroit Crownival.
MICHIGAN, AUGUST 2010

I hang up the phone and cry alone in my tent, lost and spiraling. Kitra returns in the early morning. She unzips the tent, slipping her slim frame in beside me. For a moment, I'm worried that she is one of the homeless men who have been walking up and down the alley, but I smell her and know I am safe.

"It got really crazy after you left," she tells me. "Cricket set himself on fire. His face. He's in the hospital now."

"I don't think I can do this anymore," I tell her, starting to cry.

"What do you mean?" Kitra asks, confused.

"I don't think I am cut out for this."

I feel pathetic, unable to keep pace with Kitra. I had wanted to feel at home on the road, to adapt as quickly and seamlessly as her, but I can't. It is clear I cannot. I am not safe; I am only pretending—I am not free; I am just moving.

"What can I do to make this easier?" she says.

Go away. I think. *Stop making me feel so weak.* But I don't say that. Because I am tired and sleeping in a tent in downtown Detroit with only one accomplice.

"I just want to rest," I say, and we drift off to sleep holding each other.

TWO DAYS LATER, we're back in Ann Arbor. A bloodstained tensor bandage is wrapped around Cricket's temple. He's shirtless, with the words AND WHY NOT? tattooed across his collarbone in large block letters. He's wrapped in a white sheet on the pullout couch back at THOIR. His face and body are completely covered in burns.

"Wanna kiss?" he asks me, puckering his crispy lips. "I was spinning fire," he explains. "I just used the wrong kind of gas."

Cigarette butts and crushed beer cans pepper the already crawling carpeting. Dumpster Head sits in the corner, wheezing, ball scars bulging.

I ask Cricket if I can record our conversation, and he agrees. He's been thinking about his son, Creed, and is in the mood to get a few things off his chest. As he tells me about his last time in Rainbowland, his usually jovial voice becomes trancelike, the mucus in his throat dulling his consonants. His accident has reminded him of the time his own son caught on fire, in Rainbowland, years ago.

"He darted straight to the hearth pit, and there was this hippie sitting right with his knees against the fucking rocks, and my son crawls through his knees, on his lap, into the pit. As soon as he gets to the pit he stands up and starts walking. Then I hear Amy scream, and I jolt up. I turn to see Creed, and he's up in the pit, walking. And I'm up and running. So is she, she's closer than I am. He falls on his hands and knees, and he rolls onto his side. That's why he dropped, because he didn't know what was going on, he can't understand what he's feeling."

An angry expression crosses his burnt face as he remembers the young man who didn't stop Creed from entering the pit, who just watched it all, stoned and paralyzed.

"I kicked both his kneecaps out," Cricket says. "This kid is going to be in a wheelchair or be on crutches for the rest of his life."

I'm suddenly reminded of the time Ben, my childhood neighbor, set himself on fire. When I close my eyes, I can still imagine it. Around Easter he stayed home from school and marinated his wrists, legs, arms, and cheeks in rubbing alcohol. Staring into his bathroom mirror he lit a match and watched as his human face melted off. In a gag of smoke and searing flesh, his natural fight for survival kicked in. He grabbed the shower curtain to wrap around the carnage he had created. But, because it was made of plastic, the curtain melted into the holes where his pores used to be. His skin wall turned solid.

Ben didn't die in the fire. He was left with the flesh of a tuna fish casserole: rough, speckled, red and yellow. He wore a beige bandage around his face for the first few years, flighty eyes darting out from two eyeholes. We only learned that Ben's accident was actually intentional from my cousin, Sean, who had been admitted to the hospital at the same time. They were the only two people in the burn intensive care unit. Sean had been airlifted from Northern Ontario to Toronto after setting fire to his pant leg in a freak leaf-burning mishap, a legitimate accident. I would visit my cousin sometimes, but never Ben. After all, we weren't related. When his skin healed enough to ward off infection, he took off his mask. "The boy must be really sick," my mother would say, cautioning me to stay away. "He almost dares you to look at him." But I felt for Ben—as much as someone can understand someone who sets himself on fire.

When I open my eyes, I see Cricket is staring forward, entranced by his past. When I close my eyes, I see Ben. When I close my eyes, I see everyone on fire around me. Everyone is on fire and none of them know it. My anxiety is at eleven.

"Who wants booze?" a voice interrupts, and I'm thankful to be pulled back to reality. A scruffy teen stands in the living room and Cricket awakes, saying he'll go in on it. I stand and leave the room to get some air.

Outside, I lie on my stomach on an overturned surfboard in the backyard of the Meat Mansion, trying to calm down. It's humid and I'm sweating. I desperately need to shit but can't. There's a bunch of dirty kids dozing on the patchy grass beside me, some on pieces of wood, others on busted lawn chairs: a punk rock Titanic crash. Two girls sit talking. I shift my weight to the other side of the surfboard and stray beer cans exhale underneath my body. One of the girls holds a ukulele and the other wears a frilly blue dress. It smells like noodles and feces, and I close my eyes, pretending to sleep.

"It's happened to me four times."

"It's happened to me four times, too."

I met one of the girls a few days back, when I told her she looked exactly like my mother as a child: blunt bangs, pale skin, bird eyes. She looks maybe fourteen but insists she's older.

"Everyone assumes that I'm just some teenage runaway," she said. "It's annoying."

I watch a fly wash its legs, rubbing black stick on black stick, igniting an invisible fire. It's either rubbing dirt off or rubbing it in, I can't tell. I want to sleep, but I can't calm my mind. Sal is strumming absentmindedly, singing original hymns and jingles. Kitra, sitting near me, is listening to the girls talk, too.

"The first time I was sleeping alone outside, and this guy asked if I wanted to come with them into tent village. I woke up to him putting his thing in me."

I open my eyes and sneak a glance at the speaker. Her friend nods. I feel guilty, like I'm shoplifting this story without permission, even though she's telling it publicly. Are all secrets made public when you don't have a house to store them in?

"It's just the worst when it's a friend," she continues, now visibly upset.

Sexual violence is a constant threat for many travelers. A large number of female-identified travelers have either left homes where they were sexually abused or encountered sexual abuse on the road—or both. Rape is the underlying fear whenever someone back home questions my decision to document travelers. People often ask if I don't dread the consequences of living outside, unprotected. I do, of course, but I also know that sexual abuse is rampant everywhere, not just in the traveling world. I think back to what Dharma told me in New Mexico about how every woman she has ever loved has been violated by a man, somehow. I feel horrified. I feel like I've been hit in the lower stomach.

I shut out the girl's voice and just look at her face. The frilly dress, the bird nose. Mom. *It's my mom's birthday,* I realize. *Shit, I forgot to call.*

"I don't want to talk about this anymore. Let's go get a space bag of wine."

The girls head across the street to buy a box of wine. I get up and head to the park, leaving Kitra, who still seems placid, in the yard. The Michigan air is sweating. It stinks like a sewer drain and spiders are hanging themselves from stray planks. It needs to rain but can't. I need to shit but can't. I have no privacy, no downtime, no comfort. At the convenience store, a woman and her husband are buying lottery tickets. I grab a bag of chips. The bag says *Low Calorie*. I know I'm gaining weight again. I feel self-hatred.

I walk to the park, lying my bloated body across a picnic table. I want to call my mom, but I'm too upset. I don't want to worry her. I want her to think I have my shit together. We don't talk about my travels; I keep it to myself. NO LOITERING, NO LITTER- ING, NO PEOPLE AFTER DARK. I watch a few ants struggle across the table, pulling bits of chip crumbs and foreign substances. The bugs look small but manage the weight of the food together, hunched and bent. Nowhere to go, no privacy, no escape. The table is carved with gang signs and strange names. I count the calories on the back of the bag. My stomach swells. The sky spits on me, pitifully, aching for release. No shit. The voices come back. I count the calories on the bag. *Fucking parasite.* The sky starts to pour. I stand to search for shelter. I run across the park. I'm belted with rain. I lie on the floor in the public bathroom, near the toilet. I scratch at my skin like an animal. I stare at the pubic hairs along the rim of the bowl and wonder whose they are. I force fingers down my throat. I hear the rain falling lightly on the roof. It's hitting everyone in its radius, whether their bodies are dirty or clean. I rest my head on the cold toilet bowl. *Release,* I think. *Release.*

CHAPTER 8

Trans American

(AUGUST 2010)

I NEED TO LEAVE the House of Ill Repute. I want to be outside, to be clean, to have normal conversations instead of interviewing and recording without break. A friend from back home has recommended the Michigan Womyn's Music Festival, otherwise known as Michfest, a women-only folk festival held in Hart, Michigan.

Kitra and I hear there's another, smaller event held outside the gates of Michfest, a protest site called Camp Trans, which doesn't have a $400 price tag and offers free camping and vegan food twice a day. The purpose of Camp Trans is to bring awareness to the exclusion of trans women from the Michigan Womyn's Festival. In 2010, Michfest has a policy to only allow "womyn-born womyn" inside the gates—meaning women born without dicks. One reason for this blatant discrimination against trans women, I'm told, is that the very sight of a penis, whether on a woman, man, or someone in between, is highly triggering for some of the Michfest women who have experienced sexual assault or rape.

Being politically aligned with Camp Trans's cause, and hungry for a change of scenery, Kitra and I decide to head to Hart.

Unsure of how to get to Camp Trans, we plan to hop on a bus to North Muskegon, Michigan. Twenty bucks for a Greyhound is a bit of a splurge for us, but we spend it anyway, using some of our crowdfunded money. The station toilets are busted, our bus is forty-five minutes late, and workers shout at us as we line up to pay. The building is crammed and young men look us up and down. Kitra and I buy animal crackers and eat them silently in the lobby: giraffe, lion, alligator, bear.

Greyhounds are the default form of transport for the poor American. Unlike hitching or rail riding, it is not free, but it isn't viewed as dangerous. It is simply the cheapest conventional option for folks looking to get somewhere somewhat on time for less money. The frustration in the station is palpable; few people love this form of travel.

Once aboard the bus, I squish in beside a Liberian woman en route to a family wedding. Kitra takes a seat across the aisle in front of a young mother and her screaming son. The bus is hot, the air conditioning is broken, and passengers are pissed off and surly. Personally, I feel overjoyed to be inside, headed to a place where I can sleep in a tent, find friends, and feel more like a human being for a while instead of just a journalist. As the bus pulls out, I drift off to sleep almost immediately.

I'm awoken by a sexist snarl. "Move your fat ass!"

I spy a woman in her forties wobbling down the aisle. She looks like an iguana with heavy turquoise makeup, her eyes blinking, empty. A man with a gang tattoo on his neck continues berating her.

"That bitch just sprayed vanilla perfume all over the goddamn bus! She was drinking vodka from her purse and trying to cover it up!"

Passengers turn around in their seats, whispering, checking phones. The woman seems unfazed by the public ridicule, swerving on her high heels, moving toward the front. As she passes me, I notice a foot-long knife strapped to her belt. The Iguana is armed, and she is heading for the driver. I look over to Kitra, who has her eyes focused on the mother and son behind her, who are squabbling loudly. As I try to get Kitra's attention, the mother slaps her son across the face—one resounding thwack!—and the little thing explodes into tears.

Before the Iguana can reach the driver, we hear a deafening screech, a mechanical hurl, a splash of gravel. The bus has broken down on the side of the highway, in the middle of Michigan. We're stranded with a drunk, knife-wielding woman, an abusive mother, and a number of daunting, irate gang members with neck tattoos.

"Sit tight!" the bus driver shouts to the bus.

She's thirtysomething, a stern, portly woman. She gets up, goes outside, and then locks the front door of the bus from the outside. Calmly, she begins to check the tires. I think back to the news story I heard a few months back about a carnival worker who was traveling Greyhound across Canada and was attacked by another passenger. The killer stabbed the carny and then subsequently decapitated his dead body, eating a piece of his victim's raw flesh in front of the other passengers, holding the man's head up for screaming onlookers to see.

The driver reopens the door and tells us we have a choice: to sit by the side of the highway or inside the un-air-conditioned bus. We won't be picked up for at least three hours.

"Excuse me, missus," the Iguana woman shouts at the driver. "I need my medication. It's under the bus."

"Sit down, you drunken slut!" screams the tattooed man.

"Fuck you!"

"No, fuck you, ho! You're the ho who tried to offer me a blow job!"

"I need my medication!" she shrieks, swinging her arms around, making even more visible the blade hanging from her belt.

"She's a goddamn junkie!"

"Ma'am, you really need to calm down and take a seat," the bus driver says. "Or I will call the authorities."

"They should really get her medication," Kitra says to me. "Isn't that illegal?"

"Maybe she is a junkie?" I say awkwardly.

"What difference does that make?" Kitra responds, and I feel ashamed.

Instead of allowing her access to her luggage, the driver calls the police. By the time they arrive, the woman has begun convulsing in a seizure. The police call an ambulance, which carts her shaking body away. The ambulance siren has amped up my own anxiety and I feel terribly unnerved. I lean on the wheel of the bus beside a woman whose hair has drunk so much peroxide it beams like a halo.

"Just our luck, huh?" she says. "Where you headed?"

"Muskegon. You?"

"I was on the way to my high school reunion," she tells me. "What a joke."

A few hours later, a replacement bus appears. We all board wearily and clap as it rolls on down the road. The Liberian woman beside me is in hysterics.

"I was on my way to my sister's wedding," she says. "This is not right. It is over by now."

The bus drops us in Muskegon five hours late, with no ticket refund and no place to sleep. Everything is shut down and we are at the end of the line. I complain to the bus driver, who tells us we might get a refund if we tell them what happened, but probably not.

"What, so we're just going to sleep on the street?" I ask.

She points to a brightly lit Holiday Inn across the street.

"Can I have your name?" I'm pissed off, ready to complain.

"No, you cannot."

Tats reading "Homemade" adorn the knuckles of Camp Trans performer Rocco Kayiatos.

MICHIGAN, AUGUST 2010

Kitra and I grudgingly decide to pay for the hotel from our funds and check into the cheapest room available. It is filled with what, to me at this point, are two gorgeous double beds with pristine white sheets. We take off our clothes and go in the hot tub in our underwear. We watch American television, and I have the best sleep I've had in weeks.

IN THE MORNING, we call Greyhound demanding they pay, which they eventually do when we threaten them with legal action. I think about how this approach might not have been possible for other Greyhound riders, who don't have legal connections. We have no idea how we're going to get to Camp Trans and can't find a ride anywhere online, so we decide to try our luck hitchhiking. We figure if we go out to the highway nearby we can land a ride quick, but we need to orient ourselves first.

On the main drag downtown, we meet a woman smoking a cigarette. She eyes our packs and asks where we're headed. She's young, with dyed hair and piercings, a contrast to the hyper-conservative majority of this small town. We tell her we're headed to Hart.

"How are you getting there?"

"Hitchhiking."

"Oh, Jesus Christ, girls, are you out of your fucking minds? Do you know where you are?"

Apparently, we don't.

The woman explains how dangerous it is to hitchhike in these parts, particularly on this highway. People are raped and killed on the regular, she insists. We nod and thank her for her concern, and when she sees she has not persuaded us, she offers to chauffeur us herself.

"You really don't have to," we tell her, feeling guilty. "We'll be fine."

"Don't worry about it. I'll pick up my friend and we'll have an adventure."

An hour later, we arrive at Camp Trans. Our driver drops us at the gates and hightails it out of there immediately. It is a small settlement near the gates of Michfest, with fewer than a hundred tents in rows. Topless folks traipse across the forest floor, hanging signs, chatting under pines. Expensive tents and lean-tos cover a central kitchen. I am reminded, of course, of Rainbow kitchens, but the vibe and setup are different—ovens are not built into the landscape like in Rainbowland, and all the equipment seems clunky and expensive.

As soon as we reach the entrance, we realize the vibe is shockingly militant. An angry topless individual with a small wisp of beard "greets" us. We begin to offer our names and hands but they interrupt:

"Which pronouns do you prefer?" Squinted eyes size us up suspiciously.

We stare back blankly.

"What is your pronoun preference?" we are pressed when we hesitate, more menacingly this time.

"She" Kitra says. "And she," she adds, pointing at me. I nod, terrified.

"I like to be referred to as zvi or zver," zvi says, exhaling, exasperated. "Do you mind me asking if you are cis women?"

Kitra and I stare at each other, confusedly.

Zvi looks horrified. "*Cis woman*. Meaning you're biologically born female."

"Oh, okay, then yes," Kitra responds. "And yes," she adds, nodding to me.

Zvi looks even angrier. "I just ask you to remember that this is a place for trans people, where they are not meant to feel alienated and instead understood."

"Of course," we respond. "We're here to support—"

The greeter turns and leaves us alone before we finish.

Trans-identified travelers are common on the road and at places like Rainbow. Many have been kicked out of their homes by hateful parents, churches, or communities. On the road, trans youth face a number of added pressures: bathroom restrictions, police harassment and abuse, inaccessible spaces, and the constant, enduring threat of sexual or physical abuse. Rainbow, in contrast, offers an open space to explore and assert identity publicly—and be accepted regardless of the nature of this assertion.

I was expecting to find an environment somewhat like Rainbow here, but I find nothing of the sort. The site is set up into zones: silent substance free, silent substance allowed, loud substance, and loud substance free. We choose loud substance free, mostly because it's beside a Porta Potty. As we set up our tent, it becomes shockingly clear that we are not going to get the vacation I was naively (and perhaps selfishly) seeking. Rules hang from trees. There are duties, meetings, and planned speeches with time limits. Folks are older than the dirty kids we've been living with and have significantly more money. And most use academic terminology constantly and aggressively. Having lived in a radical lesbian house, I'm used to being sensitive to others' pronouns, boundaries, and beliefs, and can appreciate (as much as any cis woman who identifies as female can) how important it is to create an equal, safe space for all gender and sexual identities. This camping setup, however, seems pretty extreme. We are required to ask before smoking, we are required to ask before sitting down beside a stranger, we are required to ask before we speak—the rules seem endless. The vibe is suffocating, especially compared to the relative social freedom of the traveling folks we've been living with. Someone has put up a sign asking if it is okay to let their dog, a small fluff ball of about ten pounds, off a leash, but someone says they are uncomfortable with it, so the dog remains bound. Even small animals can't escape blame.

"I don't understand why zvi is so mad at us," Kitra says. "Zvi doesn't know anything about us."

I agree.

That night, around the community campfire, the mood begins to improve. There are about a hundred of us milling around the fire. I meet Andy, a chatty guy from Vermont, and we hit it off talking about courses we're taking. For the first time in weeks, I speak openly, feeling I've made a friend.

"Basically I'm sick of theory," I explain, and he nods me onwards. "I want to produce. I want to trust that I am a good person and not fear that what I'm doing is offensive or an incorrect representation. I want to *do,* not talk about doing."

All my thoughts from the last few years are bubbling to the surface and I'm finally able to let them out. I know firsthand how hard it is to represent anyone at all. I've experienced, even within the last few months, angry opposition to my representations, from kids such as Kozmo and Sicka, and although I found these oppositions concerning, my resolve to stop worrying about judgment has become firmer, even when I am being judged. I need to simply focus on providing the most accurate representation I can, from my own perspective.

There is an announcement that the group meeting will soon commence. As the group gears up and sits around the fire, we discover one of the reasons the mood is so tense: the night before, during a candlelight vigil at the gates of the Michigan Womyn's Festival, a truck driver approached two members of Camp Trans, threatening them with a metal chain. Since we just arrived, we were unaware of any of the details and are caught completely in the mess of arguments, anger, and fear. We try to get details, but no one wants to talk about it. There seems to be a clear divide between the older trans women, who mostly want to let it go, and a group of younger trans men who are protesting in alliance with the trans women and want to rebel, to fight back against this oppression. The tension is palpable, and people are trying their best to facilitate conversation that is fair for all, in which everyone has a chance to speak. Unfortunately, this means the first hour of discussion is spent discussing how we are going to talk about what is going on.

"I would be willing to take stack and mediate if we decide on ground rules," says a bubbly lady, around forty years old with a short gray mushroom cut.

Andy, who is sitting beside me, explains "stack" is a way of writing down the order in which people can talk—a system of positive discourse where group consensus is met by a (to me, seemingly complex) system of hand signals.

Someone stands. "I think speakers should speak in monotone so nobody can be offended by their tone of voice."

At this point, I lose it, cracking up at the lunacy unfolding in front of me. Daggered eyes stab me. I glance at Kitra, who looks just as perplexed as I am. This campsite is a stark contrast to the house with the kids in Ann Arbor. The street kids, who many might consider to be hostile, seemed much more inclusive, more open, more accepting of difference. We go to bed after hours of discussion with no resolution.

IN THE MORNING, Kitra and I hear folks are going to a lake for a swim and we decide it would be nice to tag along and catch a bath. We get into the car of a friendly woman named Dale from Boston. Chris from Ann Arbor and Ricky, a musician from New York, pile into the car too. Finally, there's Rocco, who's devastatingly well dressed, muscular, and covered in tattoos of kittens and cupcakes. He slinks into the car seat beside me, clutching a coffee, exasperated. I stare at his beautiful leather shoes.

"Well, I am *officially* in hell." He exhales grumpily.

I feel instantly at ease in his presence. We start chatting and I tell him about our project. He says he read something similar in a magazine a little while ago, a story about kids at the Rainbow Festival.

"That was us!" I shriek. "That was our article!"

Rocco tells us he writes for and runs a magazine for trans men, a glossy publication called *Original Plumbing*, which features pinup-style photos of trans babes. He is at Camp Trans to perform a rap show the following night but is also bummed out from the heavy vibe.

"I don't get the us-versus-them attitude. I get it, a lot of fucked-up shit is going on, but why don't they want to have any fun whatsoever?"

When we reach the lake, folks remove bras and shorts to reveal scars, freckles, implants, nipples. The group wade into the water, submerging themselves, taking delight in the sheer refreshment. Dale tells me about her breast surgery and vaginoplasty, which she had done in the Philippines. Her new body is sturdy and beautiful, and I watch her in awe. I feel guilty about my own parts, that I haven't been thankful for them all along, that other people have paid good money for the bits I bitch about and scrutinize.

Kitra, realizing she is not going to get any "work" done here, folds up completely. She falls asleep in the trunk of the car on the shore. She seems to have two modes: awake and working or fully asleep. I want to relax, make normal friendships outside the project. She wants to keep working.

When we arrive back at the camp, Rocco invites us to his campsite and introduces us to Nicky Click, a curvy, bubbly lady with tattoos on her tits and a push-up bra.

"I'm not gay enough for these people!" she jokes.

Nicky begins to talk about mental institutions and wild love affairs, and I am instantly in love with her carefree, forthcoming attitude. Within minutes, I am wrestling with her, giggling maniacally, as if we've known each other our whole lives. Nicky performs later that night on the "main stage," a platform in the middle of the field. Dressed in a tiny navy polka-dot dress, she screams and whips around like a whirling dervish.

"Sex! Sex! Sex! Sex! Gangster! Little prankster! I am a fuck machine! Fuck machine! Don't call me, baby!" she screams to a sea of convulsing fans. She concludes the show after twenty minutes, after spraining her ankle during one of her stage dives.

By the end of the week, Kitra is eager to move on, and I agree. Although I'm supportive of what I perceive to be the main cause of Camp Trans, to protest the transphobic policies of Michfest, I find the setup disturbing and unproductive. Despite this, I also feel like I've been able to connect with a few new faces as a person instead of as a journalist. I feel less anxious. Rested and full of vegan food, we decide to ramble on.

CHAPTER 9

CALM

(AUGUST 2010)

'M COVERED IN spots. The doc says I have a fungal infection. When I ask her the cause she looks at me with worried eyes.

"It's just from being dirty," she says.

I also have lice and fleas. It's only been a couple weeks since Camp Trans and I'm home in Vancouver to regroup and re-medicate. My body is tired and broken down. I check on the status of my psychiatric care—I had requested to see a psychiatrist in Vancouver more than a year ago, when I first arrived—but when I find out I will not be seeing one anytime soon, I lie to the doctor, convincing her to prescribe me Adderall, ADHD medication, in addition to my anxiety pills—and fungal cream—and score myself a summer's worth of speed, paid for by the Canadian government.

Not long after this doctor visit, I'm en route to Washington State to meet Kitra and attend another regional Rainbow. Another Greyhound bus, and the similarities to my previous ride through Michigan are remarkable: the dust in the armpits of the armrests, the unidentifiable red stains on seats twenty-six to thirty-one, the bottles of blue Gatorade rolling across the floor, unclaimed and sticky. The burly vehicle carts me from place to place, from each dank, deep-fried nook to the next, completely unapologetic. Although I knew poor people ride Greyhound, I didn't realize how many kinds of poor folks there are in America. Beside me, a snarling teen with drawn-on eyebrows and Tic Tacs sits behind a Spanish-speaking Casanova in a white suit, whose eyes scan the bus seats longingly as he eats a gas station hot dog. Across the aisle sits a boy with pink nails, feeding his girlfriend cherry Pop-Tarts. The drivers, the ticket salespeople, the passengers, and everyone involved are working, riding, eating, and moving on.

Our Greyhound stops in a small town with nothing but a Starbucks. Behind the counter, a girl with a plastered-on smile hands me a sample of a sugary drink.

"Welcome to Ellisforde. If you miss the bus, enjoy your stay in Ellisforde," the bus driver remarks as we get back on.

A few passengers laugh at his nonsensical joke; most of us ignore it. The businessman across the aisle clutches a bulk bottle of Costco blood pressure medicine while reading a self-help book. On the back of the book it says *The Power of Being Here Now*.

After a few hours, we reach Spokane, my current destination. Historically, the city is a famous hop-out spot for American hobos because of its extensive railroad infrastructure. The city was once home to huge hobo jungles, makeshift encampments and impermanent home spaces erected by tramps, down by the muddy Spokane River. Many of these (mostly) men slept rough, outside, and moved to where the work was, be it lumber camp labor, seasonal work, or odd jobs. A crucial distinction between hobos and other travelers, according to historical scholar Ben Reitman, is that hobos are proud they work, and tramps and bums take pride in getting by without having to work. As Reitman puts it: "The hobo works and wanders, the tramp dreams and wanders and the bum drinks and wanders."

These days, people who still hop trains are looking more for adventure than employment. Kitra and I haven't tried it yet. Back at THOIR, we got our hands on a Crew Change Guide, the train hopper's bible, which lists times and tricks for rail yards across the USA, and we photocopied and scanned it for future use. The Crew Change is not made publicly accessible, of course; you can only snatch one from a personal contact or traveling friend, which adds to the allure of this epic document. In terms of infrastructure, instead of train cars being easy to open and accessible, like in the old days, precautions have been taken to keep people off cars—most boxes are sealed shut and many now contain surveillance cameras. Travelers, such as Scott and Spit, have warned us how dangerous it is to ride the rails, how new travelers are ruining the scene, and it's not something I am particularly looking forward to. In fact, I don't want to do it at all.

I'm crashing on the couch of some guy I found on the Internet who is originally from California. After I arrive, we sit in his living room and he plays me "Make Me a Pallet on the Floor" on his guitar, looking at me with lusty eyes. My stomach drops.

Kitra has already reached the Gathering; she's waiting for me to arrive in Spokane so that she can pick me up. On cue, my cell phone buzzes.

"I'm here." It's Kitra.

"Already?"

"Some kid drove me into town. Get ready."

I give Kitra the address and apologize to the guy for the brevity of my visit. Relieved to be leaving, I grab my bag and wait outside for the car. Finally, one drives up and a long, lean figure exits excitedly. Inside the car sit two twentysomething men I've never seen before. The driver is stoned on mushrooms and the other is passed out in the back seat, drooling.

"He busted his leg real bad," the driver explains. "He's under."

This is an understatement; he doesn't even flinch when I accidentally hit him in the face with my backpack. I apologize anyway, my Canadian accent obvious, and squish into the back with Kitra.

I'm starting to understand why kids with injuries and mental issues flock to Rainbow Gatherings, as they offer free health care at CALM, the Rainbow health center, as well as a relatively safe space to chill out and heal. Many American folks simply cannot afford doctor visits. Although Rainbow doesn't have the medical facilities to treat broken bones or any chronic conditions or ailments, they can offer herbal remedies, free medicines, condoms, love, and counseling. I have been altogether overwhelmed by the ill health of some of the nomads at the Gathering: kids constantly coughing, with fleas, infections, hepatitis, infected wounds and boils, and blood-borne illnesses.

As we drive to the Washington Rainbowland site, the car swoops and loops in the hills and valleys of Spokane. When we reach the forest, it starts to rain. We are dropped off at the first settlement we see: A-camp. Too tired to make the trek down to Main Meadow, we pitch our tent there. I'm terrified, knowing A-camp has been the site of almost all Rainbow violence, including a very recent stabbing. But rain has started pouring and Kitra sets up our tent in the grass under some high pines. I'm soaked, and when I finally drift off, I have a vivid nightmare about yelling at her at the top of my lungs.

THE NEXT MORNING, a pack of ten burly, drunken men sit at the fire pit, cracking sexist jokes and chopping up food. Surprisingly, the men are kind, if not a bit shy, when Kitra and I introduce ourselves.

"You hungry?" one asks.

Cletus, the camp cook, finds out that Kitra and I are eating vegetarian. Clad in nothing but overalls, he cooks us up a pot of dumpstered vegetables: fresh potatoes, baby carrots, beans, spinach, and cracked black pepper. As we eat—me wearily and Kitra happily—the boys discuss their love for deep-fried food, compiling a list of all the items they have deep fried in the past: peanut butter sandwiches, Oreo cookies, chicken fingers, and s'mores with cheese. The vibe is testosterone filled and boozy but not terribly intimidating, and I don't feel afraid. After a lengthy discussion about the process of deep frying bacon, someone whips out a local newspaper they picked up in Babylon that has news coverage of the Gathering. A blond man with a lazy eye and face tattoos becomes instantly heated.

"Journalists! They don't fucking get it," he starts angrily. "Fucking parasites."

Kitra and I shift awkwardly by the fire. I cast my eyes downward, watching the flames. Normally, we'd out ourselves from the get-go, but this crowd seems a bit more unpredictable, so we keep quiet and eat our food.

The man continues his tirade. "Back at regionals, some journalist asked why we all have so many dogs. I told them it's because we eat them. After that, the locals started bringing in mutts, just dropped them off with us to die."

The man, now visibly disturbed, begins rambling about how he hasn't had a bed in six years, "unless you count a squat in Vermont with thirty kids and black mold on the walls to be a bed."

His eyes are spinning backwards. I know this look. I remember it from the too-drunk kids at THOIR and Rainbows past. I know nothing fun comes from this look.

"My parents were cruel fuckers," he goes on, to nobody in particular. "They punished us by making us kneel on rice. I would never do that to a kid."

Things seem to be going a bit south and I'm beginning to feel unsafe. We pack our gear and trek down to Main Circle.

This Gathering is small, since it's a regional, not a national. There are only a couple hundred Rainbows on-site. Sitting by

Chris lies in Main Meadow, awaiting a communal dinner.
WASHINGTON, AUGUST 2010

the communal fire, I watch cats and dogs meandering, some on strings, others unleashed. Some young, some old and blind, a jigsaw of dogs, black and white, dyed bright green. A man more than six feet tall who goes by the name of Two Tall hands me a fistful of weed, then gets up and leaves me alone by the fire.

"Lovin' you, sister."

Walking down a path to Main Meadow, we spot Useless and wave excitedly. He gestures us over. He invites us to set up camp there, so we pitch our tent.

"No hugs, no bugs!" he shouts when we attempt an embrace. His hair has been cut short, evidence of a recent infestation. He looks handsome—shirtless, busy as usual.

A young girl, about nine, walks over to us; she is alone and also shirtless.

"Your momma's boobs are so big they call her Biggie Smalls," she shouts at me.

Everyone around the fire laughs, some uncomfortably, some heartily. I wonder where her parents are and feel dizzy.

A small Honda drives right across the field and up next to our tent. The two white, middle-aged Babylonians inside look confused, like they've just fallen into a parallel dimension, and in many ways, they have. I greet them with a friendly, curious smile, trying to help.

"We're looking for our daughter. Her name is Laura. She is in her twenties with dark long hair. Have you seen her?"

I apologize and tell them I haven't. I feel sorry for them. They are acting the way I imagine my parents might if they thought I ran away and joined a hippie cult. I tell them I will keep my eyes open and wish them well.

We set up our portrait booth near Montana Mud and start shooting. Looking for mainly young people, we ask passersby to take their photographs.

After a few hours, a man in his twenties, dressed like a cat, approaches me. He introduces himself as Anjel and almost immediately announces to me that he is "not gay." Although his odd statement makes me uncomfortable, his energy is innocent, and soon he is teaching me acrobatic yoga. He puts his bare feet on my hipbones and pushes upward. I'm supported and fly up high, freely, laughing. We sit down and I interview him in the burnt grass.

"I prefer 'home free,' not homeless. It's a more liberating term."

Like Cliff, Anjel has been traveling across the U.S. with a gang of bike punks. For Anjel, the nomadic life began with a traumatic event at Burning Man.

"I grew up in Florida in a beach town. Last year, I met a girl on the beach. She told me about a Burning Man event that was coming up near Tampa. It's kind of crazy cosmic synchronicity." He laughs with a flabbergasted look in his eye. "Went to the Burning Man thing. I was diagnosed bipolar and when I stay up a long time I can send myself manic, or if I go manic, I stay up a long time. So at Burning Man, I stayed up a long time, went manic. I came home and went back to a job working at a restaurant and was just going kind of crazy from sleep deprivation... I lost my job and got Baker Acted and sent to the hospital, all within twenty-four hours. Baker Acting, in Florida, is when they take you to a mental hospital when you're a harm to yourself or someone else, and they have a right to detain people for seventy-two hours. But then once you're there, the doctor can sign a thing that can hold you longer, so you kind of end up getting held against your will."

The thought horrifies me. I'm no stranger to psych wards but have never been committed against my will. In fact, being committed against my will is one of my biggest fears. I try not to think back to my own experiences, so I push them down and keep recording.

"They were talking about sending me to short-term care or long-term care because I was telling them I was sane, that I was

just playing a role, like in a movie. I was actually literally trying to play Heath Ledger's Joker, which is what scared my mom.
She thought I was going to burn her house down. Reasonable,
yeah. I would have called the cops on me too if I thought Heath
Ledger's Joker was going to burn my house down, even if it was
one of my family. I did have fantasies about, like, self-immolating,
which is when you douse yourself with kerosene and light yourself on fire."

I think back to Cricket, to Ben. Yes, I know what self-immola-
tion is, I tell him.

"I don't think I would have actually done it, but I was thinking
about it. After I got out of the hospital, I was really ready to get
out of Florida," he explains. And after some travels, he tells me,
"I went to the Rainbow Gathering in Pennsylvania. That was my
first Gathering. I like it, it's like Burning Man."

I thank Anjel for the interview and move on. I keep thinking
about fire and feel nauseous. I don't want to interview anyone
else. I just want to sit still. I just got here, but I'm already beat.

BY NIGHT, I'M relaxing by the fire, chatting with people, and a
sweet boy starts playing love songs on his guitar. An aging hippie lady hands out cookies and I take one. When a pipe is passed,
I take a toke. Listening to the guitar player, a body buzz coming
on, I lie back on a log and close my eyes. But instead of peace, I
find blackness, coldness, alien feelings.

"Kitra," I whisper. "Something's wrong."

Suddenly, my buzz has transformed: I am high, but not in a
way I can manage. I am too high. I am *way too* high. Anxiety
creeps up my neck.

"Something is not right," I mumble. "We have to get the fuck
out of here."

Kitra complies, guiding me back to our camp. I am caught in
a loop, lost, out of control: I truly feel like I am going to die. But

I can't stop laughing. Since Kitra has never taken any drugs herself, she is completely unprepared and unsure of what to do.

"Should we go to CALM?" Kitra asks.

I concede, but when we get there, it is abandoned, a hand-built stall full of Band-Aids and tincture bottles. CALM is volunteer run, so it is not entirely reliable. Also, because it is funded by donations to the Magic Hat, some CALMs are more stocked than others.

At this point, I am beginning to hallucinate, to hyperventilate, to panic. *You are going to die, you are going to die.* Kitra takes me back to our tent and lays me down. She is trying her best, but I push back. I see buildings, streams of light, figures, and childhood memories. The night is wild and on rerun, spiraling. I have lost all concept of time in the middle of a place I know nothing about, with people I know nothing about. I am howling into the dark, open abyss, mind on fire, scratching at the waxy walls of my head, my tent, my wrists, trying to grab on to something but finding nothing firm to hold on to.

"Every minute is the worst minute of my life," I keep repeating to Kitra, frantic, fearful.

She makes me drink a bottle of water, puts me in my sleeping bag. She sings to me, prayer music. I am an open vessel, pulling in energy from all around me, channeling, afraid. Then the convulsions come, the leg shakes, the deep growls emanating from inside me. I shake and shake and shake, the seizures taking over. Suddenly, I am back in my old neighborhood. I am tracing the walls and vents of the house I grew up in. I see the black vent in my bedroom. I see my childhood best friend, Kate. I am in her backyard. I see the window frames of my house, the rooms I felt anxious in, my retreats, my childhood tree house in Northern Ontario, the white birch trees. I see my own child face, wearing an alligator mask, in my basement, I'm breathing deeply, connected to the ventilating machine I was hooked onto until I was three years old. Being born two months early, I was put on a machine; the green alligator breathing mask was an attempt to make the experience less scary, though it did not succeed. I feel so unsafe, small, detached, out of control. I am weeping in Kitra's arms. I am trapped in a tent, trapped in an egg, trapped in this experience entirely. I tell Kitra I have to get out of here. I have to go home. I am afraid. I'm Babylonian. The switch has flipped. I don't want to travel anymore.

THE SUN CREEPS over the horizon and the morning comes.

"I'm leaving today," I tell Kitra, with no room for discussion.

She looks angry, hurt. We don't talk much. I trek up to A-camp to hitch a ride out, abandoning her. I tell myself I am not cut out for this. I know she will manage fine without me. Cletus is still by the fire when I reach A-camp, with his gang of boys, drinking. He shouts something unintelligible at me and I tell him I'm heading out. I stand beside his camp, holding a make-shift sign that says SPOKANE OR SOMEWHERE. A truck drives past and I see the boy who played his guitar at the campfire hop out of the back. He spots me and runs up.

"I've been looking for you!" he says. It's the first time we've talked. "Where you headed?" he asks, and I tell him I'm going home.

He tells me he wants to travel to Canada sometime soon, to play some shows. I scrawl my number and address into his notebook.

"My name is Solomon," he says, smiling, offering me a hug. "Lovin' you!" he shouts as he jumps back into the truck and takes off.

A white car pulls up the hill and I recognize the clean, middle-aged Babylonian couple—the parents I met the day before who were trying to find their daughter. I walk up to their car and greet them. They seem relieved to see a familiar face. They haven't found their daughter, and they offer me a ride out of Rainbow-land. I take it happily, hopping in the back seat.

"I don't get it," the dad, wearing coke-bottle glasses, says once we're on the road. "We used to smoke dope, we grew up in the sixties. But she's twenty-five now. She's epileptic. She can't live like that all the time. She's got to grow up."

The couple is clearly very upset, and worried about their daughter traveling the U.S. with a clan of drifters. My unshaven legs rub their beige seating, leaving stains. My boots are filthy. I tell them that I feel for them, I don't blame them, that I can't even imagine the pain they are going through. But, I say, the Rainbow Family is a lot different than they might think.

"It's not so unsafe, in comparison to lots of places she could be," I say. "It's not all about drugs."

I try to describe the positive aspects of the traveling world. I try to get them to look past the dirt, to ignore the kids who have checked out completely with booze and junk, and look at the ones truly doing it, the fast-moving ones, the ones who can sustain travel, the ones who can live freely. The parents seem calmed, because I tell them I'm educated just like them, and that, before I started traveling, I was skeptical just like them. But as I finish my speech, my words trail off and I scan the horizon. To me, my voice sounds weak and inauthentic, an echo of how it sounded before. I don't tell them I'm heading back to Babylon, that I have quit. We drive straight through Spokane. My view is speckled with fast food names: *Arby's*, *Wendy's*, *Jack in the Box*. We pass a dead dog on the side of the road, but the couple doesn't see it, so I keep it to myself. The dead dog has a halo of flies that dance and deke around its dead head, licking blood. The parents drive me to the Greyhound station, park the car, and help me find a bus. I leave an imprint of dead leaves and dirt on their cushions where I sat.

CHAPTER 10

Summer in Shangri-La

(SUMMER 2011)

THERE'S NO SOLID ground in New Orleans: the pavement shifts beneath your feet. Reeking rat corpses decay under unhinged stop signs, radioactive roaches flit in and out of open flip-flops. In places, the city is as much as sixteen feet under the sea. NOLA is alive and sweltering in the heat. It's the most enthralling place I've ever been.

It's been a year since my last Rainbow Gathering, since I've seen Kitra's face. She and I have maintained a rocky online correspondence, but we've been avoiding each other since I abandoned her in Spokane. Since then, I got a book deal to write about our travels, my life's dream, but Kitra sees this as another abandonment. As is my coping mechanism, I've channeled all my pain surrounding traveling into working obsessively. I write grant applications madly, thinking if I have financial support, then I might be able to weather the storm. Everything feels surreal and undeserved, but I grasp at the opportunity to leave the sad rain of Vancouver. I've finished my schooling, and I'm in New Orleans for the summer. I've received funding from the Canada Council to finish my book and landed a research assistantship at

Tulane University, studying the desegregation of public schools in the South. I am ecstatic.

Large numbers of travelers consider New Orleans their home base. Post-Katrina abandoned houses combined with the low cost of living and the resident population's social openness and general passion for debauchery have made NOLA a prime place for nomads to flourish. It is the veritable Shangri-La of the American traveling community. Many, if not most, American travelers have been through the Big Easy, and all of them have stories to tell.

"People come and people go, and I don't know what for." A voice I know bursts down Decatur Street. "People come and people go, and I don't know what for."

It's my first day in the city, and Sal's is the first familiar face I see. I dash up to him like a child at a Christmas mall. He's in front of Rouses Supermarket, near Royal Street. A group of tourists surround him, dollar bills in hand, and a swarm of unfamiliar traveling kids sit around his stoop. He finishes his slippery song, not flinching or missing a note, and turns around to greet me.

"How are you, my love?" he exclaims, like it hasn't been almost two years since we've seen each other.

THAT NIGHT, I rent a room at the Royal Inn, where Charles Bukowski lived and worked. A messy *Hank Was Here* is carved into the dirty wall, marking his territory.

Kitra calls me from Portland. "How do you get hep C, exactly?" she asks me.

Her new boyfriend has hepatitis and she doesn't want to get sick. She's been put up in a house in Austin, Texas, by *National Geographic* to do a story. She's tramping on her downtime, continuing the story without me. I find out she's fallen in with Fat Kids Kitchen, a nomadic collective that travels around the U.S. dumpster diving and feeding poor people for free. I feel a pang of jealousy. The distance between us is palpable, but we're better than we were before. She tells me that Josh, Maray's boyfriend from Ann Arbor, has been arrested, though I don't know why, and is serving time in a Nevada prison.

I can't imagine this young, sensitive boy in the custody of a federal institution. I start writing him in prison, sending him love notes. His imprisonment reminds me of the faulty justice system, a system that criminalizes homelessness and poverty. In Bill Boyarsky's three-part series for *Truthdig*, he explains that poor Americans are often jailed for the most petty of offences, "such as jaywalking, refusing to move their possessions from the sidewalk, urinating in an alley or sleeping in a public place." Like my friends who were called faggots and niggers back in Ann Arbor, jailed for eating chicken by the river and skinny-dipping. In *No Safe Place: The Criminalization of Homelessness in U.S. Cities*, the National Law Center on Homelessness & Poverty expands on this point: "There are some activities so fundamental to human existence that it defies common sense that they might be treated as crimes. Falling asleep, standing still, and sitting down, are all necessary actions for any human being's survival. While these activities are unquestionably legal when performed indoors, more and more communities across the country are treating these life-sustaining behaviors as criminal acts when performed in public places by people with nowhere else to go."

I email Kitra to tell her I've been feeling down.

"You were depressed on the road, and you're depressed at home. I don't think it has anything to do with geography."

She is correct. I try not to email her again. While I'm working, writing, and missing my friends, punk kids are getting shot in the Katrina-decimated Ninth Ward. Eight train hoppers died in a warehouse fire in the same area their barrel fire burnt over. I see their faces on the TV, in my dreams, on my Internet feeds. I wonder if I know any of them, but I don't recognize their real names. I read a detailed description of events on the

Times-Picayune website: "New Orleans' deadliest blaze in decades took the lives of eight squatters who were trying to keep warm by huddling around an open fire in an abandoned 9th Ward building on one of the coldest nights of the year. Authorities said the death toll in the fire was the largest since the Upstairs Lounge fire in June 1973, when 32 people died in a second-story bar in the French Quarter. The Orleans Parish coroner's office had yet to identify the victims, five men and three women, by Tuesday evening. Chief investigator John Gagliano said the agency had some 'good leads' and will obtain the help of a dentist to assist with identifications, as the bodies were badly burned. Most of the people who died did not live permanently in New Orleans, he said. A survivor of the blaze told firefighters that the people staying in the building were squatters, most of them in their teens and early 20s."

I'M COMING DOWN off my Adderall, and some manic kid I just met is demanding to read my tarot cards. His name is Nelson, and like me, he's new to New Orleans. I'm staying at a house in the Bywater, a slowly gentrifying hipster haven. I found my host, Laura Borealis, a pedicab driver and local activist, on the Couchsurfing website, as did Nelson. I haven't found an apartment yet, and I'm hoping to meet travelers before I settle in.

"You ever heard of nutria?" he says, holding a can of Lucky Lager, eyes swirling unnervingly. He spreads the flashy cards on the couch I want to be sleeping on. "It's an animal. Like, half-rat, half-beaver."

I've spent the last week sustaining myself on a diet of shrimp, carbohydrates, and stimulants. I'm in a sweltering, alien city where I know no one very well, and my patience is wearing thin.

"No," I tell Nelson. "I have never heard of nutria."

"They live in the swamps. The State of Louisiana is paying people to kill them. Four bucks a head."

I ask Nelson why the government would do that. He explains they are bad news for the bayous. The pests, also known as coypu, are an invasive species and apparently chewed down the levees so badly that they even had an effect on Hurricane Katrina, he says. They have become such a problem that the American federal government spends $2 million annually to help eradicate them.

Parasites, I think. His dealt tarot cards stare me down: Five of Pentacles, Three of Cups. The Empress.

"You will lose money, estate. You will lose inspiration. You will be seen as a trickster, a temptress. You will be surrounded by poverty."

"I'm going to sleep now," I tell Nelson curtly, and he picks up his cards and bikes off into the heaving evening.

"SO GLAD TO meet you, darling!" my new landlady exclaims, offering me a chubby Louisiana hug. A beefy black mutt accompanies her, panting. "Welcome to your new home!"

I'm renting a basement apartment that I found on Craigslist. It's in the Seventh Ward, a low-rent, high-crime area full of funky, colored shotgun houses crammed with people.

"We only have one rule," my landlady tells me solemnly.

I can only assume the plural pronoun includes her dogs, as she lives alone.

"Always, *always* remember to lock the side gate."

Her eyes turn away from me, to the street. A cop car passes by, a young man on a bike, another cop car, an SUV belting bounce music.

"Once, a truck drove through my driveway, right through the gate. It killed four of my baby puppies. Killed them dead."

Her eyes glaze over like scum on a can of soup.

"I can still hear their little bodies hitting the car. *Thwack, thwack, thwack.*" She imitates the sound of a puppy being slain by a Chevy.

"I'll be sure to lock it," I tell her, disturbed.

She looks at me too long, then regains her composure. "Thanks so much, darling. Well, get settled. I will see you in the morning."

I need to get some exercise. I unlock the bike I bought earlier in the day from a shifty man uptown selling bikes from his yard.

"Where are you going?" my landlady asks, opening her front door when she sees me outside.

"Out?" I respond, confused.

"At this hour?" she says, nervously looking around. "Around here?"

It's nine in the evening. I bike off without answering. I stop at a McDonald's and stuff myself. I shove the food down as quick as I can, and it's greasy and revolting. I bike back, avoiding eye contact with everyone, afraid of the dark moving shapes surrounding me. I don't know anyone and my landlady's comments begin to haunt me.

Back at the house, I close the blinds to the driveway and try to relax. I unload my books onto the shelf. I write in my journal. I lie down on my bed. In the ensuing silence, I hear the scurrying, the punctuation of pin-thin legs on linoleum. I walk to the kitchen and turn on the light: the scurrying stops. A shiny black cockroach the size of a dime stares up at me. She wriggles her tentacles. I flick on all lights in the kitchen, in the bathroom, in the bedroom. I turn on the light above the stove and a bug as long as my index finger falls from above the vent, landing in the cooking element, flailing, writhing, shrieking. I jump back, repulsed. *Parasites. Everywhere.* Suddenly I see swarms of insects coating the walls and floors, bumps of black tar on the wallpaper, seething and screaming. *Am I hallucinating?* My mind and gut are shrieking and it doesn't matter—all that matters is that I must leave this place immediately. I snatch my pack, my books, my belongings and run outside. In the darkness, I see bugs in the gutters, on my steps, on the pavement, crawling up my new blue bike. *The vermin are everywhere.* I hail a cab and head back to the Bywater.

AFTER CRASHING ON couches for a while, I sublet an uptown apartment belonging to a friend from McGill. It is far beyond my budget, but bug-free. The neighborhood is still shady at night, but during the day, wealthy inhabitants flock from Whole Foods to Pinkberry, frozen yogurt and organic oranges in hand. My previous landlady refuses to give me back any of my rent money or deposit, claiming I fabricated the bugs.

"I take pride in my house and my business. There are no roaches. Not one."

I don't have the energy to fight. A huge chunk of my funds sinks down the drain. When I return to her place to pick up my bike, I find it gone. When I ask about it, she tells me, suspiciously, that "things disappear here."

I cloister myself in my new house, trying to force myself to write. I schedule deadlines. I buy Post-it notes. I question the presence of roaches. Am I hallucinating? I see nobody. I spend time at Tulane, transcribing interviews with black women about their experience desegregating schools as girls. I take archive photos of civil rights activists' scrapbooks and wonder what I am doing with my life. *You will lose money, estate. You will lose inspiration. You will be seen as a trickster, a temptress.* I question myself, my project—if I even have a right to write about traveling culture, if I'm a fake, an oogle, a bloodsucking tick.

There is a radical right-wing group papering the city with flyers, saying the Bible forecasts the world will end in a week. My parents, newly retired public school teachers, book a flight to New Orleans for a visit. I think of how many travelers don't have folks, and instead of lucky, I feel guilty. When they arrive, we talk about my research. As usual, there is a lot we don't talk about.

We leave the traveling stuff alone. They take me on a riverboat tour of the Mississippi, an old steamboat converted into a tourist trap that holds hundreds of British and Canadian tourists for an hour. They feed us tilapia and bread pudding while we bop along to a live jazz band. I eat quickly, taking no breaths.

The captain comes on the loudspeaker. "I want to thank you for taking this trip, despite the dangerous weather conditions."

My parents laugh nervously. Old folks shift in penny loafers. I scan the water for eyes.

Back on land, my father loads up on Hand Grenade cocktails on Bourbon Street, going buck wild. I stay in their clean hotel room, watching *Star Trek*. Their presence is comforting.

And then, out of the blue, I receive an email from Kitra. She is in Memphis, with some traveling kids.

"I'm thinking about heading west. Then maybe NOLA," she says.

She still feels a million miles away, even though it's less than five hundred.

NELSON SHUFFLES THE deck again and I cut the cards, holding my breath. He lays the cards out like sparkling fingernails, a full hand. We're at cafe Envie in the French Quarter, and he is reading my tarot cards for the second time. Despite our rocky start, he's one of my only "friends" in the city, one of the only people I see.

The Hermit, Ace of Pentacles. The Chariot. King of Swords, King of Pentacles. Success, power, newfound direction.

"You can make a lot of money off this project you're working on," he begins. "But your biggest fear is selling out."

"No it isn't," I snap, offended, bordering on angry.

"Okay, it's not."

I'm still suspicious of Nelson. I don't like his predictions, the way his eyes turn, his short stature, his nervousness. He reminds

Laura Borealis bikes into the heaving heat of a Louisiana summer night.
NEW ORLEANS, AUGUST 2011

me of myself. I take more Adderall to compensate. I look up nutria on the Internet. There is a hipster clothing line, garments made exclusively from the vermin's skin. It is called "righteous fur," and they say their clothes are made of "ethically killed" animals. The site has photos of bearded young people wearing shaggy ponchos and caps. Their line's goal is "to help control a destructive invasive species; to raise public awareness about the need to restore our vanishing coast; and to provide a stylish guilt-free alternative to traditional fur products."

Nelson wants to meet up again a few days later. He says it's important. We meet at a coffee shop uptown.

"I think I was raped," he tells me once I've biked there. "And maybe drugged, too."

His eyes are spinning—the wrong way. He tells me he's kidding, he wasn't raped, he wasn't drugged, it's a joke. I don't get it. He's stuttering. I'm unnerved. I begin to wonder if he's schizophrenic, or if he's just been seeing things in the city like I have. After our coffee, I avoid his phone calls.

JACQ IS WEARING an American-flag belly top, tied tight around a push-up bra.

"Delicious," she proclaims, sucking back a blob of deep-fried dough.

The staff at the diner gave us a free order of hush puppies, fried dough dripping with nacho cheese.

"I love this country," she concludes. "Don't you?"

I haven't seen Jacq since undergrad. After studying Russian at McGill, she came out, moved to Brooklyn, and found work taking her clothes off in strip joints.

"I cater to a niche market at the club 'cause I don't spray tan," she tells me, her milky skin luminous.

We are at a diner down the road from our campsite. Inside, there are tattooed crucifixes on the walls and on our waitress's wrist and the back of her neck, as well as decapitated deer and shiny brass plaques everywhere. Violent hunting scenes run incessantly on the TV: *GUN SHOW, BIG BUCK, SHOOT 2 KILL*.

Three of my friends from home have come to visit me for a road trip. Our destination is Idapalooza, a queer faerie festival in backwoods Tennessee, a haven for wandering and wild LGBTQ2 folks. I need a reprieve from New Orleans—it's hot, lonesome, and overwhelming. We've cramped into Jacq's friend Mal's red Pontiac. My roommate from McGill, Kai, is also along for the ride.

"Oh!" our waitress exclaims, bringing me my plastic dinner basket. "I didn't notice your nose ring when you came in!"

I smudge my septum with a greasy forefinger and laugh nervously. The waitress brings us two extra slices of frozen millionaire pie, a pineapple–cream cheese concoction topped with whipped cream, on the house.

"Here you go, darlings. I hope you enjoy."

We suck the food up.

"Y'all come back now!" she yells as we leave the restaurant, and we stifle laughter.

After dinner, we head to our roadside campsite at Lake Bogue Homa, which provides tent sites and access to toilets. Mal and Jacq, now in matching American-flag crop tops, crack Buds and belch into the sweaty night. I cuddle with Kai in our tent.

Rocco, the rapper I met at Camp Trans, calls me from New York. I talk to him sitting wrapped in an orange tarp, staring out into the Bogue Homa swamp.

"You're going to Ida?" he asks, sounding emphatically unimpressed. "Have fun with the chiggers."

Chiggers, I learn, are invasive bugs that are plentiful in Tennessee. The bugs burrow and weave, venture under vulnerable flesh, nestling under follicles, making your body their home.

"There was a time in my life where I wanted to live in a van and travel all the time," he tells me. "But I think that time has passed."

Rocco lets me know that he's recently broken up with his girl-friend, which I assume is the reason for his call. His tells me his psychic predicted his next girlfriend would be a short blond with a sunny aura. I'm more than a little skeptical, but obviously interested. We set up a date for him to fly to New Orleans for a visit.

In the morning, I get up early and the white walls of the Bogue Homa washroom are covered with a skin of bugs. Stray shits lie fermenting in unflushed toilets; unkempt shower curtains hang like limp ghosts. We load the car and keep driving to Ida.

"NOW!" THE LARGE woman holding the microphone screams. She is dressed as Daria, the sardonic cult nineties TV character, and she is lying, splayed open, in a metal wheelbarrow. "I'm going to need you to piss on me *right now!*"

I look to Kai beside me: he is stone eyed, mouth agape, staring intently at his own knee. To my amazement, a huge green bullfrog sits atop his kneecap. Kai looks perplexed.

The woman onstage continues shouting insistently. "Come on, you fucking queers! Piss on me! What's wrong with you?"

A few bodies tentatively approach the stage, unbuttoning pants, pulling up dresses.

"What's up with the frog?" I whisper to Kai, pointing to his knee, and he shakes his shaved head as the thing hops off.

"Why can't anyone pee?" he whispers back, pointing to the stage of nervous queers.

Suddenly, one topaz urine stream emerges, then another, and another still. The crowd erupts in laughter and applause, an ecstatic and bawdy shriek. The performance piece is over. It's clear from the workshops and circulating literature that the majority of these folks are politically engaged, yet they manage to maintain an inclusive and jovial vibe. I laugh, thinking Camp Trans could have taken a note from this free-spirited community. I don't interview anyone and try to enjoy myself instead.

"Where's Jacq?" I ask.

"Did you check the Gay Gardens?" Kai responds. "Or the S&M barn?"

Later that night, dancing near-nude to bounce music, I shout into the sky, ecstatic. It's the most fun I've had in months.

BACK IN NEW Orleans, I try to work but can't find my words. I'm refreshed by the reprieve from writing and researching, but it's still sweltering and I'm alone again.

Rocco visits, serving as a welcome romantic distraction. I take him out on the bayou on an alligator tour. We watch as our tour guide feeds the crocs sugary marshmallows. Their bloated bodies approach our boat and I think how unhealthy these snacks must be for the creatures, whose diet should consist of other wildlife: birds, fish, river rats. Their lazy prehistoric bodies float down the river as our boat leaks gas into their habitat. Their wildness is deflated by sugar.

Things with Rocco go south fairly quickly: he's not into hitching or road dogging, he's in AA and I'm very clearly not, having spent the last few months up to my eyeballs in booze and speed. It's obvious we're traveling very different paths. On our last night together, I make a disparaging comment about a fictionalized prostitute character on television, and Rocco yells at me until I leave the room to weep alone in the shower. He apologizes, we make amends, and he flies back to New York in the morning.

I contact Sal and bike down to the Bywater to see where he's living. I find a run-down house in an abandoned part of town, adjacent to the railroad tracks. I have to call Sal on the phone so that he can let me in. He's all smiles, same purple vest and tattoos and *Voodoo* hands, calm as ever. He leads me to his backyard.

"I've got chickens!" he exclaims, but I don't see any in the dark. "I'm cooking a big pot of jambalaya!"

A brood of snarling punks sit on his back porch, smoking cigarettes and staring into space. Sucking on a peach daiquiri I bought on the corner, I smile and try to act friendly. Sal ducks into the house to check on his stew. I tell them I'm new in town. I offer them a sip of my peach daiquiri, and they snicker.

"Daiquiris. They're like crawfish, or beignets. You have to do them once," one of them says.

"Or you don't," snaps another individual. "How do you like it here?" they ask me curtly, smirking.

I shrug. "People are a little mean," I say.

I know I'm an outsider here. Despite being instantly enamored with the city, I know I haven't put in the time yet. I am a newbie in a place where newbies are particularly common and very much despised.

"They're tough," they respond. "Be careful," they continue, pointing to the daiquiri in my hand. "Those things are 90 percent proof. One gave me a UTI once."

The group has a stifled laugh at my expense. I crawl into the kitchen, embarrassed. Sal welcomes me. He's tending to a teeming pot of jambalaya on the stove, seemingly unaware of the travelers on his porch. I look around his shabby, ramshackle fort. He lights a joint and gives it to me.

"I'm really into cooking these days," he says, offering me a scoop of brown goo.

I help Sal clean up the kitchen, wipe his greasy table with a greasy cloth, watch him dump the bucket of water acting as a makeshift sink into a smeared toilet bowl. We sit together at his kitchen table and I tell him my troubles: how things with Kitra have deteriorated, how I feel fake and lost.

"I guess I need more stability." I explain that this embarrasses me, makes me feel weak and phony.

"I've done the traveling thing for years," he says. "Now I like to have my own bed, my own pillow. I get it."

I ask him how his music is coming along.

"You didn't hear? *Rolling Stone* magazine was doing a cross-country street performer contest. Another band came first, but they didn't claim it. I came in second, so I won. Out of the whole city! That's why I'm trying to stay here for a while. To see if people will pay me to play music."

I feel so proud of him, so happy that he has been recognized for his raw talent.

"So many people will have something to say about what I'm doing, that it's selling out, but it's not. I have to surround myself with people *doing* things. They're just talking shit 'cause they don't have anything else going on."

I tell him I understand. Sal mentions that, like Kitra and me, he and Eli also had a rift.

"He doesn't want to make money, or have fame, or be known. He is doing his gruff, punk thing. I'm happy for him. It's sad, though. I haven't found anyone else I can collaborate like that with. We were magical together."

I nod in agreement.

"Kitra got in contact with me," he adds nonchalantly. "She's hopping trains now." Sal lights the roach, takes a hit. "She's really doing it, huh?"

My heart sinks. I'm shocked. "I didn't know she was riding trains."

"That's what she said."

Sal gets up to use the washroom and I'm left alone in the room. *Has she taken that final step?* A cockroach, big as a mouse, flies in through the open door, landing on the fridge. I freeze, petrified, paranoid. At first, I'm not sure it's real. I try to ignore it. *You are safe. You are okay.* As I relax, it flies back out the door, and Sal returns. He finishes off his joint and we head out together to meet his friends at St. Roch Tavern. Outside, as we mount our bikes and turn the corner, a clanging sign slumps down in our path, reading RAILWAY X-ING. A train a mile long splays out in front of us, a moving billboard. Graffiti letters turn cursive as it speeds by.

"So I found this baby bird the other day, while busking on Frenchmen," Sal shouts to me over the clang of the engine. "It had fallen out of its nest. So I picked him up and put him on my hat. I started busking with him just sitting on my head."

My laugh is caught up in the bustle of the train. Sal's silk vest flaps. He tightens his tattooed hands on his handlebars.

"Then, one of the palm readers from the square came by to tip me a dollar for my song, and she said, 'Hey kid, you got a bird on your head!' 'Yeah, I know' I said, 'I found it on the ground. I was thinking I might take care of it.' I mean, we have some birdseed and stuff at the house for the chickens. But before I could say that, the palm reader lady tells me she raises baby birds at home. She took it with her, nursed it back to health."

I imagine the young pink thing, kicked out of the sky before its time, exposed but chirping, alone.

"The lady came back to tell me it flew away fine."

The train cuts the path beyond into blurry squares. The road is framed and re-framed in bright, colorful boxcars. The world turns to soup on the other side. I wonder if Kitra is on board, if she has made one car her new home. We bike onwards, and I don't look back.

CHAPTER 11

Moonflower

(AUGUST 2011)

JACQ STANDS IN the desert night, naked save for a beige thong. She's shameless and unafraid, white arms spread wide and slathered in gold glitter and Vaseline. Atop her head sits an oversized hamburger hat—puffed yellow buns, brown patty, and a plush pickle like an outstretched tongue. Her body glitters in the Nevada moonlight. The electronic music backbeats thump heavy, but the night feels silent in her presence.

I'm back at Burning Man. I flew into San Francisco and drove here with Jacq and her friend Paolo, a handsome surfer bro from San Francisco. It's the end of the summer; my work at Tulane is over. I'm back at the Burn because I don't know where else to go, who to live with, or how to live correctly anymore. I want to be around nomads but am feeling sick of Rainbowland. Writing has been horrible. I'm getting nowhere with the book but convince myself Burning Man will inspire me. I'm running out of money but haven't thought about what will happen when it's gone. I figure I will be fine, even if I don't have anything: the freedom from worrying about the future is one gift traveling has given me.

Jacq picks sparkles from her manicured nails and flicks them into the night. I watch her body move and feel better about myself, far away from responsibilities, free.

"**LET US BEGIN** by calling in the chakras," the pseudo-guru in the white dashiki says. "Lam Vam Ram Yam Ham Om."

I've left Jacq cooking hot dogs at our camp. A man named Dashiki is leading a free seminar that promises to teach his students to overcome anxiety through breathing exercises. It's held in a white yurt near our campsite. I'm wilted, exhausted from the previous night. Jacq and I spent hours ecstatic and alive, dancing atop cars, thrusting our bodies against the desert night, high and flapping. Now, sober and hungover, I'm attending the workshop to calm myself down, to start following the tips that mental health professionals and professionally healthy folks have bestowed upon me.

Mist sprays from the top of the yurt. We sit in a circle. There are elderly nudists, a middle-aged woman wearing an afghan, and a topless teenage girl with acrylic eyes painted atop her breasts.

"Lam Vam Ram Yam Ham Om."

I take up the chant.

"Lam Vam Ram Yam Ham Om."

Dashiki pulls out a small tube. "This is a mixture. It contains moonflower," he tells us, perched in the center of our circle. "It will help clear your nasal passageways, help you to relax."

I've never heard of moonflower but assume it's a harmless plant, akin to elderflower or echinacea. I figure it can't be any worse than what I ingested the night before. I try to look past his L.A.-wanker aura and squirt the tasteless liquid onto my tongue.

Dashiki gives us a new phrase to chant in unison: "I am happiness. I am full acceptance. I am equanimity."

I chant along. "I am happiness. I am full acceptance. I am equanimity."

I can feel my fingers tingling and suspect I must be doing something "right."

I start chanting a little too enthusiastically. "I am happiness. I am full acceptance. I am equanimity."

The tingling spreads up into my wrists.

"I am happiness. I am full acceptance. I am equanimity."

Suddenly, I realize I've forgotten the meaning of the word equanimity. I scan my mental dictionary, but my mind feels white, blank, hard-shelled. *Equanimity. Equanimity. Equanimity.*

"Look in the eyes of those around you," Dashiki instructs us. "You are looking at everyone who has ever existed."

All I see are the eyes of others: tearing, winking, watching. Eyes on limbs, foreheads, breasts. Eyelashes fluttering on breasts. I think about Kitra, how much I miss her. Then I think of nothing at all. Dashiki mentions something about the Pleiades star cluster, sacred languages, and other things that don't make sense. My mind whitens, flips frantic, starts to spiral. Eyes open, watching, winking, fluttering on breasts. My head bashes backwards on the desert floor, my arms flail up. Within seconds, nothing sounds like language: I'm in full seizure. The tingling in my limbs has turned to cramping. My arms and legs snap into my body like a crab retracting its claws. I am on my back, gaze stuck upward, eyes wide open. I can hear a woman screaming, the gasps of exasperated hippies. I don't listen; I just look up. There's a hole in the yurt, so I can see the desert sun. No distractions. Nothing to think about. The sky looks serene: blue, clean, calm. No clouds. Someone asks me to release. A moment of peace comes over me. My limbs stop shaking and I am nothing but calm, nothing but release, nothing but "yes" and "sure" and "okay." I'm open even to Dashiki, who sits beside me like a robed vulture.

"You really let go of a lot there, sister," he says, patting my shoulder.

A small water pipe breaks at the top of the yurt and a stream begins to drip directly onto my face. I don't ask myself if I'm

Conditions for entry to the Traveling Titty-Totter of Terror, a massive art installation at Burning Man, include being topless.
BLACK ROCK CITY, AUGUST 2011

hallucinating because I have lost the capacity to question. My mouth fills with water from above. I drink freely.

"Did everyone see that?" Dashiki whispers dramatically. "The fairies are helping her through this tough release," he announces to the crowd.

I laugh at the lunacy of his statement, at our bizarre shared predicament, but nobody notices my response. Fully cracked, I laugh and laugh and laugh, but no one seems to notice; they're too busy focusing on their own fairies.

Moonflower (*Datura stramonium*), I later find out, is a mind-altering entheogen that has been used for centuries by shamans and mystics. Moonflower has been nicknamed the "suicide plant" for its tendency to drive those who consume it to madness and self-harm. It causes amnesia, so those who ingest it often forget that they've done so. It is also called "Jamestown weed," named after Jamestown, Virginia, where, during Bacon's Rebellion in 1676, some British soldiers accidentally ate the plant. According to historian Robert Beverley's 1705 book *The History and Present State of Virginia*, the soldiers went insane for the next eleven days. The plant is a nocturnal species. Night-blooming petals splay open in the moonlight, waiting to be pollinated by lunar moths.

Moths, like burners, are lunar beings; they follow the light of the moon. For the past hundred years, moths have been dying in enormous numbers. Electricity has perverted their flight paths. Some scholars believe that, instead of following the moon as their horizon point—as moths had done for millennia—they now fly to any light source available. One by one, junkies of luminance cut loose from the pack and nose-dive into traffic lights and neon signs. Moths swarm at night, smashing their fragile frames against bright, hot bulbs, diving into flames, committing certain suicide.

DURING MY FIRST visit to the Burning Man urgent care clinic, I'm treated by a woman in a naughty nurse outfit, who gives me two cups of Gatorade and tells me to chug. Many of the staff are nurses and medics volunteering their time. The unit is a collapsible fort with thick walls to keep out dust. There are rows of cots filled with overdone burners—mostly on bad trips but some bleeding.

On my second visit several hours later, after stumbling around the desert aimlessly, I'm hooked up to a freezing IV bag, laid back on a stained lawn chair, and told to "chill out." After a few hours, they release me back into the desert.

Back at camp, I approach Jacq, who is lounging in lawn chairs with her Aussie ex-girlfriend.

"I feel really fucked up, man," I say. "I'm really fucked up."

"Darling, you're fine! You're wonderful!" Jacq smiles, turning her face back to her company, leaving me alone.

As the day melts on, I'm gripped by an angry, alien sense of doom. People don't look like people. *This is not normal,* the voices say. *You are not safe. You are not okay.* Then the most dangerous one: *You are finally losing your mind.* By this time, my memory of ingesting the moonflower is all but gone, and I decide, since the medical facilities aren't helping and there are no buses leaving the festival, to barricade myself in my tent and try to relax.

"Lam, Vam, Ram, Yam, Ham, Om," I hum to myself.

It doesn't work, only elevates my anxiety, reminds me of the seizures, the weirdness, the pain.

"Ram, Bam, Ham, Spam."

The calm is gone, and inside my tiny plastic tent in the middle of the desert, I'm gripped by a type of panic I have never experienced before. I'm burning up. The music won't stop. And the thoughts, the thoughts, the thoughts. I hit my head with closed fists—the only way I can think of to stop the looping, bug-eyed thoughts. I hit and hit, but they don't stop, and neither does the incessant hum outside my tent. The hive, the bass, the brass, the swaying vulgarity of men and women dressed in neon thongs. I can feel the Gatorade and IV saline bulging in my bladder. *You're a parasite. You're fucking crazy. And now you are going to piss your pants.* Too terrified to leave the safety of my tent, I empty a two-pound jar of cashews and almonds onto the floor, pull down my pants, and piss into the jar convulsively. Small husks and shells float, suspended in the hot yellow liquid, tiny planets trapped in an ether of urine. Perched above a nut jar, weeping, I realize I am too far gone. I unzip my tent.

"I'm scared I'm going to hurt myself," I tell my friend Anna, a fellow writer I know from back in Vancouver, who is sitting outside my tent. "And I don't know why."

The third time I arrive at the clinic, it is in an ambulance. Inside the screaming vehicle, a paramedic asks me soft questions: "Do you have a history of anxiety? Mental illness? Allergies? What's your mother's first name? Is this your first time in Nevada?"

I'm still taking my anxiety pills but think back to all the other, less legal ones I've downed in the past few days. The paramedic attaches a blood pressure gauge to my shaking arm and pumps.

"Have you always had high blood pressure?"

This is not CALM. This is something very different. They take me to the Sanctuary—Burning Man's mental health ward. It is shaped like a hexagon. This is where the creepiest, frothing freaks end up, where volunteers named Elmo feed you shrimp Cup-a-Soups and bathe you in psychobabble. No amount of Gatorade in the world can save you here.

I'm tucked into a camping cot and covered in a rainbow blanket. All of my friends are gone. I am alone in a dome in the desert. Sick people are scattered across the room—stoners, burnouts, burnt bodies with white bandages and bloodied heads. For the next twelve hours, I dip in and out of shaky consciousness.

I'M AWOKEN IN the middle of the night by firecrackers. In the Sanctuary, I can hear them but not see them. I imagine tiny bursts of electricity in the black sky. In my mind, they're shimmering purple insects, shot willy-nilly, luminous. Comfort comes as the fireworks blast on, louder and hotter and more filled with fire. I do not fight them; I allow total obliteration. My mind, my body, my eyes are gone. I have burnt up entirely. I have lost everything I have ever known. The pangs of anxiety subside, and I feel peaceful. Dead or alive, cocooned in a tacky rainbow comforter, surrounded by sleeping visionaries and vicious seers, I take a deep breath.

CHAPTER 12

Gator Nation

(FEBRUARY 2012)

"**Y**OU SLEEPING OUTSIDE tonight?" strangers with face tats and packs ask me.

I'm walking the streets of New York City with a stuffed army pack. I have less than a hundred dollars in my bank account. After the moonflower incident, I returned to Toronto to get my head on straight. I was sleeping in Terra's extra room, working part time at a tea shop. But I knew I needed to travel in America alone; I felt it was important for the book, and for me personally.

Here in New York, I plan to stay with a friend from university named Jesse. I meet Jesse at a fancy bar where I can't afford to drink. He laughs at my ragged clothes and bulging backpack. I've come a long way since he saw me last. At Jesse's place, I watch his friends with blunt bangs and expensive clothing do cocaine and complain. They look at me like I am an oddity and ask very few questions. I spend the night on Jesse's mattress on the floor, where we cuddle until I fall asleep.

From New York, I take another bus to Richmond, Virginia, where I meet up with Solomon, the boy I met playing his guitar at the campfire at Washington regionals before I left Kitra. We've kept in touch online. He's currently living with his folks on a goat farm, where he makes his own cheese. He has agreed to give me a lift to the winter Rainbow Gathering in Ocala, Florida. I wait at the rank Richmond bus station, the night encroaching, as angry, frightening Americans argue and smoke around me. He finally picks me up, hours late, after dark, in a vw camper van. Sitting shotgun is Atom, a monotoned, ginger-haired hippie from D.C., who has recently discovered his distaste for mainstream American culture through the Occupy Wall Street movement.

"I live in an intentional community now," he informs me.

"Congrats," I respond, unintentionally sarcastic. I realize I sound disingenuous, skeptical. I quickly backpedal. I make small talk. I fake smile. Although it's tiring, I know agreeability is a desirable trait while traveling. These strangers are my only family now.

THE FOLLOWING MORNING, the three of us drive to Rainbowland in the camper van, which Solomon calls the Blue Dragon. His wacky ride is rammed to the windows with oddities: colorful crystals, fossilized badger knuckles, bubbling jars of fermented kombucha. A lone deer skull sits in the trunk, jangling back and forth.

"Cacao?" Solomon asks me, filling my crumpled palm with tiny purple nibs. "Really antioxidant rich."

I've given this young man dominion over my diet, being both broke and disposed to dietary self-neglect. He's packed a cooler: cabbage, carrots, dandelion greens, browning sprouts, and nutritional yeast—food mostly homegrown or bought on food stamps—and I eat whatever he hands me.

"Hold tight, darling," Solomon says. "We're headed home."

Through Blue Dragon's cracked windowpanes, I watch burnt pines and swamp-side trailer parks, billboards for liposuction and discount implants, *OUR SAVIOR CHRIST*, and *CHRIST*

ALMIGHTY! I insist we stop off Interstate 95 at a popular tourist trap called South of the Border. Solomon looks horrified. He's a health food junkie and the signs advertise everything fried. The parking lot is deserted. Vibrant racist ads hang from stray posts: one sign shows a sombrero-wearing man being pantsed by the gnarled jaws of an emerald-green alligator. The cactus-font caption beneath reads *Reptile Lagoon.* Inside the artificial lagoon, prehistoric creatures sit in cages: Nile, Slender Snout, the Great American. Yellow eyes wide under lime-green halogen lights: predators on display. It makes me sad. Babylon has its head on backwards, and I long for home.

When we stop for gas near Ocala, we are confronted by a middle-aged man.

"You kids be careful on the road," he says suspiciously, eyeing Solomon, who is pumping gas barefoot on the asphalt. "The police won't hesitate to stop you."

Solomon nods.

We drive on, stoned and unafraid. Nobody stops us.

After a few hours, we arrive at Ocala National Forest, and Solomon parks the Blue Dragon at its edge. Handwritten banners hang triumphantly across the forest entrance: *WORLD PEACE* and *WE LOVE YOU* and *WELCOME HOME.* The rows of cars, as always, are endless: multicolored bliss mobiles, Frankenstein RVs, Blue Bird buses. There are notably fewer cars than I'm used to seeing, and I assume it's because it's February. I've never been to a winter Rainbow before, but both Spit and Scott have told me it's where the real road dogs congregate, the twenty-four-hour travelers.

We hop out of the Blue Dragon. A never-ending stream of filthy, barely covered bodies, mostly male, emerges from the forest. A few naked babies run amok, blond and cherubic, mugs smeared in swampy mud. An enormous pile of soiled clothes, rags, blankets, and tops glitters with flies and ticks. Above it, a sign says *FREE.*

Home, I think. *Is this home?*

A convoy of cops and rangers in green uniforms flank the forest entrance. A few smirk, men licking their chops, but the majority of them look afraid and confused. They avoid eye contact, shove stubby hands in tight uniforms, and exchange nervous glances. Most Rainbows pay almost no attention to the police presence whatsoever.

We strap on our backpacks and enter Rainbowland by dirt path.

ALLEN, IN HIS forties, has long blond hair and a pet pit bull that he keeps chained to a tree. His tent is behind ours, and in the morning, his dog—her name is Lady—barks incessantly, awakening all in earshot.

"Come over here, girlie," Allen tells me, leading me to his green plastic tent.

He pulls her out: a small alligator with slick black skin. The gator's yellow eyes tick back and forth, like a windup clock. She looks both fragile and ferocious.

"I caught her near the swamp," he says, proud of his bounty.

I think back to South of the Border, back to Paige's pet at the House of Ill Repute, the plaid-skinned gator she kept in that gurgling plastic coffin, that stinking enclosure that slowly domesticated the wild creature, made her bored, tamed her into submission. I smile nervously and return to my tent. I'm sleeping with Solomon for company.

On the forest floor outside my tent stands a dirty tramp, holding up a sloppily skinned alligator carcass.

"Who killed this?" he shouts accusingly, raising the skin sheet like a misplaced poncho.

Another filthy man at the fire, curled around a whimpering mutt, fesses up.

"We was outta dumpstered food." He laughs. "We had to resort to primal instincts!"

Someone reminds him that hunting American alligators is a felony in Florida.

The man with the mutt simply looks at him, chuckling. "Yeah, well, I have multiple felonies."

I find many of the men at the gathering—and it is mostly men in attendance—are either running from the law or have recently been let out of jail and can't find work because of their records. This revolving door of imprisonment and freedom is something a whole realm of Rainbows experience on a daily basis.

Within days, the limits of sanity have melted off entirely. I realize this is not a safe place, and at this point in my travels, that is saying a lot. Pits of buff men huff inhalants, bad trippers shout at invisible sun gods, large groups of men suck hoses of the hallucinogen DMT communally, nodding off in the midday sun. A man named Captain Jack speaks alluringly to a group of teenage girls, regaling them with tales of his recent meth deals turned sour. Unlike the other Gatherings I have attended with Kitra, this one seems to be composed largely of angry, drugged-out felons.

I sit by a fire and scribble in my book, frantically. I don't interview anyone. I think back to Skunk's words, back in New York, on Brighton Beach: "People are parasites," he'd said. "They're a bad thing, altogether."

By day six, Allen goes missing. Everyone asks where we'd seen him last.

"It's not like him to leave his dog like that," they say of Lady, who remains chained to the tree, barking maniacally. "The police must have finally gotten him."

I worry more about the alligator, trapped in that small plastic tent, baking in the February heat, her teeth sharp enough to chew through plastic walls but probably unaware of her own power. I understand this feeling.

STANDING BY THE swamp is a young girl with eyes like saucers of milk. The swamp—a gelatinous mud hole—has become a makeshift bathing station for all Rainbows on-site; that is, all Rainbows brave enough to bathe among alligators. The swamp girl looks dazed, angelic. Glowing, she paws at her protruding tummy. She tells me she's six months pregnant. I try to guess how old she is (sixteen, seventeen?), if she has a family back home, if there is a "home." I ask her if she's afraid. She doesn't answer me. She's not wearing shoes. Her toes etch gullies in the silt. She says she's heard of a birthing method where the umbilical cord isn't cut but left to detach naturally.

"Sounds dangerous," I say.

The girl looks at me as though I've misunderstood.

"No," she says. "It's not dangerous."

I wonder how many other experiences I have dismissed out of fear.

Another bather, Mother Gaia, bathes in the gator swamp every afternoon. She removes all her clothing and enters by way of a fallen stump. Whoever is there—whether she knows them or not—rushes to help her in and out of the murky water. She doesn't ask for their assistance but takes it when it's offered. I watch her bathe. I don't know how Mother Gaia got to the Gathering, whether she's camped alone or with others. It's clear, once you've watched her long enough, or attempted to engage her, that she is dealing with some form of dementia. Her walk is unsteady and her arms have weakened with age. At first, I'd worried for her safety: her bare, exposed, elderly flesh, open to the elements. But then I see how the Rainbows, even these Rainbows, always rush to help her.

After I've observed her for a short time, she nods to me, and I follow behind her from the shore. I balance my bare feet on a soggy stump, disrobe, and ease my naked body into the swamp. On the shore, tattooed men and strangers look on. I submerge

Friends stoke flames around the campfire at Fat Kids Camp.
FLORIDA, FEBRUARY 2012

myself entirely. Sunlight penetrates my weary form, water cradles me. Beside Mother Gaia, I feel safe; I feel stable and unafraid. She smiles at me, skin luminescent, eyes like glue pots, still, and I smile back, ecstatic. I wade in the weight of her grace. When Mother Gaia bathes in the gator pond, no pests dare swim near.

THERE'S A MAN in winter Rainbowland who believes he is eternally trapped in an egg. Egg Man will never be sober again.

"I'm in the egg," he screams when he's agitated. "I'm trapped in the *fucking egg*!"

Maybe he's done too many bad drugs, maybe he's been to too many Rainbows—who knows?

When it's nighttime and the dirty kids have come out to play, smoking weed, smooching, hanging in hammocks beneath the stars, Egg Man approaches and tries to engage us in dialogue. The smart kids pretend they don't hear him. The seasoned kids don't acknowledge him at all: they avert their glare, talk loudly among themselves, take off to another campfire, leaving Egg Man muttering to himself. But I can't look away. Like most of the weird shit I've seen traveling, he transfixes me.

"Help me," he says. "I can't get out."

When I remain speechless, he repeats himself loudly, then screams, then convulses, out of reach entirely.

"I CAN'T GET OUT!"

"OH, I'VE DONE time in the pen," a man mumbles beside me, a maniacal gasp-grunt aimed at nobody in particular.

He sports drooping sweatpants beneath a sagging gut, stretched skin exposed. He has a long and almost clownish mop of curls, hair that dances deliriously around his halo of a bald spot. He sits down beside me on a log.

"They accused me of butt rape."

The man isn't, as far as I can tell, talking to anyone, but his body is angled to the girl beside me, a lady traveler I've just met. I'm caught off guard by his comment. My heart dips underwater. I watch the man focus his energy on the girl, his gaze like dirty beams, a conveyor belt of confusing information. The traveling girl, avoiding eye contact, looks confused, and then suddenly, out of nowhere, starts singing, fearlessly. I eye my tent, not twenty feet from us. There are no locked doors in Rainbowland. Beside me on the forest floor, Solomon strums chords. He accompanies her song. Defiantly, she sings, unwilling to partake in this predator's expression of maniacal humanity. I close my eyes and began to sing, too, softly, off key, along with my kin. I feel the saggy man's eyes land on me momentarily. I feel the weight of his muddled vision. I try to stop thinking. I look the man directly in the eyes. My voice comes out clear, soft, then surprisingly defiant. We look at each other sadly. The man, deflated but notably calmer, stands and wades off into the murky afternoon. The woman, seemingly satisfied, shakes off the experience, like a duck that's too wet.

"You all right?" I ask her, interrupting her song.

"What do you mean?" she responds.

"That man, I thought—"

"I'm just fine," she says, cutting me off. Her voice is earnest. "I'm just fine."

Meanwhile, Egg Man is yelling in the forest, screaming at the sun gods.

THAT NIGHT, SOLOMON and I hang crystals from the poles of our tent, citrine and quartz to keep the bad energy out. We decide to make love—a brief, divine spark of ecstasy—and afterwards, he tells me that he doesn't want a relationship. He loves me, but he's got future travels ahead. He can't be tied down. Feeling burnt, I leave the tent and head out into the dark woods alone. Another road dog gone. I came here, to Ocala, for freedom, for travel, for adventure—but now I am not sure of what I am doing. Solomon's detachment annoys me, and my own longings surprise me.

Dazed, I walk to Fat Kids Kitchen. It's the same camp Kitra was traveling with when we last spoke. Jacob, a skinny traveling kid, is at the grill, cooking food. He has placid blue eyes, shaggy teeth, and holes in his earlobes three inches wide. I walk up to him, sad and hesitant, and he motions for me to join him.

"Wash your hands," he says softly.

He gives me onions and carrots to cut, and I chop them all, silently. We spend the day working. I ask if anyone has seen a photographer girl named Kitra. One of the kids beside the fire says I just missed her, that she was here only days ago but has since moved on. At sunset, we bring our buckets of stew to Main Circle to feed the masses. There are hundreds of bodies there, dancing, yelling, singing, screaming. A man wearing ceremonial garb marks my forehead with red face paint. I feel the high of the communal celebration, but I'm warier this time. I know this is not New Mexico. I've been burnt too badly. I sit in the grass, letting Jacob put an arm around me.

I head back to Fat Kids with him to sit in the sky net with the group. The sky net is a hangout built six feet up in the pines, constructed from the seatbelts of abandoned cars. It fits ten kids, and in it we swing and laugh, smoking pot and sharing zuzus. I stare into the sky. Jacob holds my hand innocently. I look up from my comfortable perch in the sky net to see Egg Man, right beside us. His eyes are fixed on me, swirling backwards, definitely the wrong way. His hair is a confusion of fuzz. He stands up, balancing on the seatbelt grid of the sky net, placing his legs carefully as he approaches me. I'm trapped. He starts mumbling, gesturing toward me, grasping, lunging. Jacob doesn't seem to notice. I try to stand, but the seatbelt net is unsteady and my legs wobble. Panicking, I thrust myself down toward the forest floor, landing with a thud, a large thump I feel through my shins. Then I stand up and run. I run and run and run, blood coursing through my legs. I run and run and run, because it's what I've learned to do while traveling, to keep moving forward, to make the world blur around me when I don't know what else to do. The acid in my legs burns. I keep running until I can't any longer.

Jacob catches up behind me, panting. "Hey! You all right?"

I don't answer and he doesn't push. He puts his arm around me and we keep walking. He asks if I want to come back to his tent and I nod. In the darkness we reach a fork in the dirt path where we are confronted by two ominous white shapes, glowing in the night.

"Check it out!" Jacob laughs, grabbing the white forms.

I realize what I'm looking at and laugh, too. Two pristine white pillows lie on the ground, side by side, luminous in the moonlight. I think about Dharma, back in New Mexico. "To be free you've got to give up your pillow," she'd told me.

We grab one of the pillows to share and leave the other behind for someone else to discover. Avoiding my tent, we walk in the dark to Jacob's home: a green tarp pulled over a sleeping bag. He has a guitar, a collection of crystals, and can of beans.

"Sorry it's not much," he says. "And watch for vomit. I was sick yesterday."

We lie down in his sleeping bag. We watch the stars through the tears in the tarp, scratch our bites, talk quietly. He tells me after Ocala he's headed down to NASCAR; he's got a gig picking up trash.

"You could come with me," he suggests. "It's pretty good money."

I could do that, I think. *I could do that. Or I could just go home.*

I feel the soft pillow beneath my head; it is a comfort I will no longer deny myself. Comfortable, outside, I fall asleep under the stars.

IN THE MORNING, I convince Solomon to drive me back to Babylon. In the light of day, I realize the trip is over. I've missed Kitra, and although I've proved I'm able, I don't want to travel alone anymore. I don't want to do this anymore at all. I've seen enough and have enough material to finish the book. I know I'm not a full-time nomad; I never have been, and I never will be.

From the Blue Dragon, we wave good-bye to the loonies and babies and burnt pines. Along the way, we pick up a trio of train hoppers, two young boys and a girl, who are covered in soot and looking to hop out. We drop them near the tracks. They give us chicken they paid for with food stamps. Solomon drives me to Gainesville, a college town a few hours from the Ocala site. I know my godsister, Lauren, is living there and I haven't seen her for a long time. We show up at her door late—hungry, soiled, swamp faced.

"Jesus Christ!" she exclaims, holding me. "You are absolutely filthy. Are you okay? What the hell happened to you?"

I look down at my limbs. I know my skin is home to pests and possible parasites, scary critters that are part of me now.

"Nothing," I respond, earnestly. "I'm just fine."

Solomon showers and spends the night, and in the morning, he hugs me and drives south.

My godsister spends an hour picking deer ticks from my body with clean metal tweezers, tiny bloody backpacks on my thighs and stomach and pelvis.

"You might have Lyme disease," she says softly, telling me I have to get checked out.

I shower twice, but the mud won't come off.

The next day, Lauren drives me around town in her Toyota. She's been living in Florida for a few years now, working as a bat biologist for a conservation organization. I slink into her clean car, rub my rump against the monochrome interior, clip on my seatbelt. We listen to the radio. I watch the trains roll along the tracks beside us with no urge to follow. The local university sports team, the Florida Gators, have made the play-offs, and the city is painted red, green, and blue in their honor.

"Football is a big thing here," she says. "America is pretty weird."

I nod in agreement.

As we drive, my eyes dart back and forth between the signs for fast food joints, their ads salacious and cartoonish: *2 breasts, 2 thighs for $2.99.* I'm assaulted by insane depictions of the human frame on billboards, blown up, scrawled upon. Plastic road signs, plastic containers by the roadside, plastic waste everywhere. On the highway, we drive by an ad featuring a busty blonde in short shorts that read *Gator State*, her tanned buttocks hanging high in the air like fleshy targets, her doe eyes almost entirely cropped from the frame. Underneath, the caption reads GATOR NATION. I glance at my godsister behind the wheel, someone I grew up with—not blood, but family. I think back to our days as children, our summers on the lake, swimming naked and unafraid, free among white birch trees. Now my skin is filthy, weathered, thick: reptilian. My stomach growls and we stop for food. I feed myself until fulfillment.

Back in the car, heading north, I slit my eyes, lick my chops, and sink back into the dull, buzzing traffic. I smell like life experience. I long for stillness. The road ahead is endless.

Reintegration

I T'S BEEN ALMOST four years since I found myself covered in ticks after leaving the Ocala National Forest, six since I first fell into Rainbowland. Time travels differently for different people. For me, the nomadic life proved unsustainable. I burnt myself out big time. Tail between my legs, I returned to Toronto with a racing mind and busted body. I *had* a safe place to come home to—a privilege most folks I met on the road do not have. In Canada, I deloused, had my blood tested for hepatitis, and medicated the mass of fungus growing atop my skin. All of these procedures and remedies were covered by the Canadian health care system. In the pillow of this privilege, I returned and, slowly, reintegrated. I became Babylonian again.

Restrictive social norms are more obvious once you've been free of them. Often, I long for, and romanticize, the old life I touched the surface of while traveling. I detest paying rent and holding a time-consuming job. I abhor attending cocktail parties in condominiums and making small talk with people who don't care about anything real. I long for the blazing wildness I experienced firsthand. I miss the unconditional acceptance of Rainbowland.

I felt free on the road but not safe. I was terrified of the omnipresent violence, of the carnage of poverty, the nastiness of the American underbelly. The majority of travelers I met were traveling because they wanted a way out. They were pursuing the dream of freedom, often in the face of poverty. As Scott told me back at the House of Ill Repute: "I had a choice. I could have been a methamphetamine addict. But I decided to do this instead." I believe this to be a positive choice.

I feel pressure to offer a grand revelation about nomadic America, but I'm more sunk in wonder. I understand the appeal of leaving Babylon for as long as possible. With the world crumbling around us, it's liberating to move fast, to get lost, to feel the ground underfoot. When you're slow, and still enough, you can feel your skin burning, your eyes turning; you can see all the memories you'd rather forget. I do know a few things I didn't know before: that it is possible to live without money, that successful forms of anarchistic governance do exist, that cops should never be trusted, that peaceful protest can be effective, and that we can accept everyone unconditionally. Anyone, and everyone, can become family. I do not overlook how important Rainbowland is in holding this space of possibility. Traveling can make a person both fatalistic and optimistic. You learn how to be fully present—profoundly present—in the good times, and you move forward when things go south. But as Kitra asserts in her recent TED Talk, entitled A *Glimpse of Life on the Road,* "No one loses their inner demons by taking to the road."

One can make cages out of any setting, any situation. These days I feel most free in stillness, in prayer, in solitude. On the road, I experienced life-changing lows and accessed a joy I had never experienced before—dancing in the rain at the Prayer for Peace, soaking in the swamp beside Mother Gaia. Nowadays, I suckle on these memories constantly for strength. I listen to my *Dirty Kids* interviews with awe, an awe that grows and grows the more I stand still.

ACKNOWLEDGMENTS

MANY FOLKS MADE *Dirty Kids* possible. Thank you Andreas Schroeder, my thesis advisor, for encouraging my voice and propelling me forward. Thanks to the Greystone Books team for believing in this project, and my editor Jennifer Croll and copyeditor, Shirarose Wilensky, for the positive and meticulous guidance. Thanks to the Social Sciences and Humanities Research Council and Canada Arts Council for their ongoing financial assistance. Jay Torrence, Anna Maxymiw, Emily Urness, Kaitlin Fontana, Kim Fu, Sigal Samuel, Andrea Bennett, Indrapramit Das, Taylor Brown-Evans, Kevin Spenst, Erika Thorkelson, and the rest of the UBC drunkards—I am grateful for your inspired feedback and friendship. To my witches, Kai Bick, Zach Stanley, Val Lippman, Carla Figucia, and Jacqueline Frances, and to my Vancouver family, Tzvi Tal, Ari Lazer, Chris Telford, Hannah Sea, Krystal Patience, and all the kind souls from Tzvi's Place—I am forever indebted. Thanks to Keith Urquhart, Joel Brown, and Ivan Roberts Davis for the earliest edits and to everyone who offered me valuable advice through this long process. To my family, god family, and Kew Beach friends: thank you for gifting me with a stable home and for supporting my writing.

Our travels would have been a lot harder without the funds raised through Kickstarter, so thank you to everyone who donated, especially: Erin Ellis, Bidi Dworkin, Dagmar W.M.,

Paul Lowe, David Graham, Melissa Sawatsky, Adam Witten, Judy Knie, L. Murphy, Margaret, Erin Ellis, Peter Komlos, Josh Clavir, Barbara Soalheiro, David Rheingold, Janice Rubin, Peter and Triene Lower, Edouard Olszewski, Dale Edwards, Forrester Hambrecht, Barb and Doug Hooton, Ian Urquhart and Cheryl Powell, Josh Haner, Gay Block, Helene Klodawsky, Don Tate, Daniel Sieradski, Bia Fiuza, Cristina Jane, Sylvia and Paul Knie, and Karen Cahana. Thank you to Kitra, who walks with angels.

Finally, my biggest thanks goes out to the travelers I interviewed for *Dirty Kids*—all the road dogs, drifters, and Rainbows I met along the way.

REFERENCES

Anderson, Nial. 2005. *A Study into Hobo Literature*. Glamorgan, U.K.: University of Glamorgan.

Beverley, Robert. 2013. *The History and Present State of Virginia*. Williamsburg, VA: Omohundro Institute of Early American History and Culture.

Brodie, Mike. 2013. *A Period of Juvenile Prosperity*. Santa Fe, NM: Twin Palms Publishers.

Davies, W.H. 2011. *Autobiography of a Super-Tramp*. New York: Melville House Books.

Kerouac, Jack. 1997. *On the Road*. New York: Viking.

Moore, Alan, and David Lloyd (illustrator). 2009. *V for Vendetta*. Burbank, CA: DC Comics.

National Law Center on Homelessness & Poverty. 2014. *No Safe Place: The Criminalization of Homelessness in U.S. Cities*. Washington, D.C.

Niman, Michael I. 2003. *People of the Rainbow: A Nomadic Utopia*. Knoxville, TN: University of Tennessee Press.

Reitman, Ben Lewis. 1989. *Ben Lewis Reitman Papers*. Chicago: University of Illinois at Chicago.

Taylor, Chris. 2014. "Burning Man Isn't What You Think, and Never Has Been." mashable.com/2014/08/22/burning-man-2014/#sXjNxcFfr5qi.

Urquhart, Chris, and Kitra Cahana (photographs). 2010. "The Rainbows." *COLORS* 76 Teenagers: 36–43.

Vollmann, William T. 2008. *Riding toward Everywhere.* New York: Harper Perennial.